EXCEPTION

EXCEPTION

A Texas County's Dream
for Realizing Juvenile Justice

Greg Sumpter

Fort Worth, Texas

Library of Congress Cataloging-in-Publication Data

Names: Sumpter, Gregory, 1970- author.
Title: Exception : a Texas county's dream for realizing juvenile justice / Gregory
Sumpter.
Description: Fort Worth, Texas : TCU Press, [2016]
Identifiers: LCCN 2015047570 (print) | LCCN 2015048611 (ebook) | ISBN
9780875655802 (alk. paper) | ISBN 9780875656298 ()
Subjects: LCSH: Juvenile corrections--Texas--Tarrant County. | Juvenile
delinquents--Texas--Tarrant County. | Juvenile justice, Administration of--Texas-
-Tarrant County.
Classification: LCC HV9105.T44 S86 2016 (print) | LCC HV9105.T44 (ebook)
| DDC 364.3609764/531--dc23
LC record available at http://lccn.loc.gov/2015047570

TCU Box 298300
Fort Worth, Texas 76129
817.257.7822
www.prs.tcu.edu
To order books: 1.800.826.8911

Design by FUSION29

This book is dedicated to Rhett and Luke,
who further my vision of the dream.

This work is also a tribute to the life and work of the
late and Honorable Judge Scott Dean Moore.

EXCEPTION: An instance or case not conforming to the general rule

Contents

Foreword

William S. Bush
Texas A&M University-San Antonio

Juvenile justice is an inherently local endeavor, administered by judges, probation officers, and staff members elected or appointed at the city or county levels. It is easy to lose sight of this essential fact among the media reports of abuse scandals in juvenile correctional facilities and administrative shake-ups in statewide juvenile justice agencies. Even the recent "pay for play" scandal in the state of Pennsylvania, in which a juvenile court judge was convicted of sentencing youths to a private facility for which he received financial benefits, can mislead observers into perceiving juvenile justice as an obscure process that takes place at some distant level of the state or federal bureaucracy. Invisible to all but the children and families who come into contact with them, the staff members and professionals who have devoted their lives to juvenile justice remain tied and ultimately accountable to their communities. They rarely receive public attention unless something has gone terribly wrong, and therefore are widely viewed in a negative light. Local in its administration, juvenile justice typically and ironically goes unnoticed by most of the members of the local community.

This phenomenon is reflected in much of the historical literature. National and statewide surveys tend to synthesize local experiences while glossing over the personalities and incidents that have shaped distinctive juvenile justice agencies. Meanwhile, more focused studies of urban juvenile justice systems in cities such as Chicago, Milwaukee, Boston, Los Angeles, and Memphis often provide in-depth analyses of specific time periods such as the Progressive Era that were formative or pivotal in the history of juvenile justice. Moreover, the authorial voice in these studies tends to be that of the historian; rare indeed has been the historical study of juvenile justice written by a practitioner or ex-practitioner.

For all the above reasons, this book's title, *Exception*, is especially appropriate. The author, a longtime juvenile probation officer, is able to present a historical narrative from a unique perspective. As a practitioner, Greg Sumpter is attuned to the daily challenges that juvenile justice professionals face; the triumphs as well as the pitfalls inform his view of juvenile justice history. *Exception* also represents the first published historical study of a local juvenile justice system in a major metropolitan area in the state of Texas. Its broad chronological sweep affords the reader an opportunity to discern change over an extended time period. Readers may debate the extent to which the Tarrant County experience truly diverges from other localities in Texas, but they nevertheless will learn about key individuals such as Judge Scott Moore, a maverick juvenile court judge whose efforts helped lead to reforms in the statewide administration of juvenile justice and the founding of the Court Appointed Special Advocate (CASA) program. Through Moore and others, this book argues that an emphasis on juvenile rehabilitation, and a stubborn insistence on viewing juveniles as vulnerable and malleable adolescents rather than fully responsible adults, made Fort Worth exceptional.

Exception tells a local story set amid shifting tides at the state and national levels. It should provide an impetus for more close studies of juvenile justice systems in Texas cities. This book's publication comes at an especially relevant moment in juvenile justice history, when the historical pendulum has swung toward emphasizing rehabilitation over punishment. At the time of this writing, the State of Texas is rapidly shifting authority, resources, and the kids themselves out of large, isolated state facilities and back to the cities and counties, under the assumption that superior and more cost-effective rehabilitative treatment can be found at the local level. In order for this enterprise to succeed, then, the "exception" chronicled in these pages will need to become the rule.

Dr. William S. Bush is the author of *Who Gets a Childhood? Race and Juvenile Justice in Twentieth-Century Texas*.

Preface

This book was initially not a book at all but an attempt to present and preserve the history of Tarrant County Juvenile Services to the staff, in an effort to look at where we have been and where we are going. As this work continued, the volume of information began to mount. It also became apparent that the history of the last four directors was fairly comprehensive, but the decades prior to the 1950s were almost unknown. Tales had been told about the department being exceptional in some ways, with no real accounting of why the claims were made. This book was written in an attempt to give an account and to tell this story.

Research included personal interviews with many of the career employees and retired employees of the department (well over thirty individuals) and searches of history available from all corners, including archived newspaper documentation. This is the story of Tarrant County Juvenile Services. Any and all royalties from the sale of this book will go to the Court Appointed Special Advocates (CASA) of Tarrant County (http://www.speakupforachild.org), an organization founded by Judge Scott Moore.

Acknowledgments

I'm very grateful to the many people whose guidance and information were invaluable in creating this book. These included:

In-person interviews with: Riley Shaw, Jerry Wood, Charles Vermersch, Alfred Briones, Don Dalton, Sandra Williams, Marihelen Wieberg, Judge Jean Boyd, Judge Tim Menikos, Judge Ellen Smith, Judge Kim Brown, Mayor (at the time of interview) Mike Moncrief, Gerald Ray, Bill West, Carey Cockerell, Lyn Willis, Mike Morrow, Vickie Bowers, Bennie Medlin, Judge James Teel.

Telephone interviews with: Cookie Baker, Cherie Townsend, Vickie Spriggs, Lynn Ross Jr., Delores Hogans, Robert Woodert, Ellen Tyler, Charly Skaggs, Sudie Graham, Ray Pierce, Toby Goodman, Nancy Janice, Bill Austin, Sam Schonafeld, Mel Brown, Nancy Moore, Sharon Fuller, Patsy Thomas, Gladys Carrión.

Juvenile Justice:
Is It a Dream Unrealized?

From its inception, the dream has been to have a system separate from adults, one with the ultimate goal of rehabilitation. The history of juvenile justice is riddled with dashed dreams and broken promises. Calls for reform preceded the creation of a separate court, and those calls for reform of the system have only gotten stronger with time. As much as there is a desire to have a separate and distinct system, history is replete with examples of adults turning juvenile justice into a miniature adult system.

There are calls now by some reformers to abolish the entire premise of juvenile court. Some say it should be completely redone. Others feel that juveniles should do adult time for adult crime, and yet still others feel that juveniles could be tried in adult court with all of their current protections in place but face a separate sentencing model based on age.

The movie *Inception* is a story about planting an idea, a dream, inside someone's mind so that they begin to believe that it is their own idea. Early in the movie, Dom Cobb, the lead character played by Leonardo DiCaprio, says, "What is the most resilient parasite? Bacteria? A virus? An intestinal worm? An idea. Resilient . . . highly contagious. Once an idea has taken hold of the brain it's almost impossible to eradicate. An idea that is fully formed, fully understood—that sticks; right in there somewhere (pointing to his head)." Cobb defends the idea of inception when a colleague suggests it is not possible. The juvenile justice arena seems to keep asking this question: Is the idea—the dream—of juvenile justice impossible to fulfill?[1]

1

What does it mean to dream of juvenile justice? There is always the risk that those who hear someone else's idea will take it to an unintended place. The reformers who originally generated the idea of juvenile justice have planted an idea that has defined and changed those who have taken up the cause of the founders. The system would be different from the adult system and would operate like a "kind and just parent." This idea has changed forever what is seen as acceptable and unacceptable in the treatment and rehabilitation of youth who come in contact with the system.

Much of the idea of a juvenile court was borrowed from English law. When the Children Bill was under debate in the UK House of Commons in 1908, this defense was made by a supporter of the measure: "We want to say to the child that if the world, or the world's law, has not been your friend in the past, it shall be now. We say that it is the duty of this parliament and that this parliament is determined to lift, if possible, and rescue him, to shut the prison door, and to open the door of hope."[2] According to an *El Paso Herald* article from 1910, Judge Julian Mack, Chicago juvenile court, would later say, "We are not opening the door of hope" to the delinquent when we "fail not merely to uproot the wrong, but to implant in the place of it, the positive good. We must study thoroughly the underlying causes of juvenile delinquency."[3]

In 1909, that same judge, Julian Mack, one of the first judges to preside over the nation's first juvenile court in Cook County, Illinois, described the goals of the juvenile court:

> The child who must be brought into court should, of course, be made to know that he is face to face with the power of the state, but he should at the same time, and more emphatically, be made to feel that he is the object of its care and solicitude. The ordinary trappings of the courtroom are out of place in such hearings. The judge on a bench, looking down upon the boy standing at the bar, can never evoke a proper sympathetic spirit. Seated at a desk, with the child at his side, where he can on occasion put his arm around his shoulder and draw the lad to him, the judge, while losing none of his judicial dignity, will gain immensely in the effectiveness of his work.[4]

Over one hundred years later, we still struggle to realize that dream. Is it possible to do so? Recent headlines drawing public attention to instances where we have fallen short, where youth have been abused within the confines of the very system charged with protecting them, seem to suggest that although the goal hasn't been attained, it might yet be won. Calls for reform continue, with some state systems, including Texas's system, continuing to be overhauled and redirected toward the original dream. How do we get to where we want to go? Why is the road paved with more disappointment than hope for a better future?

This book attempts to tell the story of the people and places responsible for Tarrant County Juvenile Services. Storytelling is a process of orally passing on narratives of our history from one generation to another. Storytelling, at its core, is primarily about places and people. When we hear the stories of others, it helps us refine, measure, and complete our own stories. It gives us a sense of connectedness to an even bigger story. Everyone longs for a sense of where they have come from, and where they are going. There is a quote by British historian Thomas Babington Macaulay that succinctly states the importance of this kind of storytelling: "A people which takes no pride in the noble achievements of remote ancestors will never achieve anything worthy to be remembered with pride by remote descendants."[5]

Tarrant County, Texas, has had a juvenile court since 1907, some eight years after the original juvenile court's inception in Chicago, Cook County, Illinois. Tarrant County is believed to have established the first such juvenile court in the state. From the beginning, the Tarrant County Juvenile Court has been viewed as a system that others should follow. This book reviews the troubled history of juvenile justice, in particular its history in Texas, and compares that to the trajectory of juvenile justice in a county where the motto is "the perfect mix of cowboys and culture." Perhaps within the story of Tarrant County Juvenile Services there is a model for others to follow toward the fulfillment of the original dream. The seed has been planted.

ONE

Juvenile Justice History: National and State

This chapter scans the history of juvenile justice systems at large, with particular attention to juvenile justice in Texas. It is intended to frame the history of the particular system in Tarrant County, and is in no way intended to be an exhaustive recounting. There are other books, including the one written by the author of the foreword, which have already covered this work. It is impossible to tell the story of Tarrant County juvenile justice, however, without describing the trajectory of the system at large. The dream is bigger than one county and even one state.

The Shoemaker

There was an early recognition in dealing with crimes and consequences that young people should be treated differently from their adult counterparts, but the line between adults and juveniles has been blurred over the course of history. In England's common law, there was this understanding of separateness, and it was assumed that the same line of separation would apply to all. The only way to draw that line would be by looking at a person's birth date. If delinquents were below a certain age, they were not held responsible for their actions. If they were above a certain age, punishment was prescribed, even if that meant the individuals were removed from society. There was also an age range where their culpability could be questioned and different remedies could be attempted. This identification of a particular age has at times been arbitrary, a gut feeling about who knows the difference between right and wrong and who deserves to be institutionalized. More recently, including by advocacy groups in upcoming legislative work in Texas, there are calls to raise the age of culpability based on research in adolescent brain development. This attempt to

4

determine justice based on age would become the framework for justice and rehabilitation for juveniles in the United States.

John Augustus, a shoemaker in Boston, Massachusetts, is widely heralded as the "father of probation." In early America, prior to his efforts, punishment was often the primary solution when laws were broken. In 1841, Augustus convinced a judge to release an adult drunk to his supervision in lieu of sentencing him to jail, and he brought a sober and changed man back to court in three weeks. His services came into demand, and Augustus would often sit in court and make decisions about which individuals he truly thought he could help. In 1843, he began to work primarily with young people, after offering voluntary probation services to three teenagers who were caught stealing. He soon had the care of thirty children at a time.

Why would a man who made and repaired shoes get involved with the outliers of society, whom the court would typically oblige by sending to prison? He was concerned that those committing petty offenses were being given similar punishments to those from whom the public needed protection. He eventually determined that young people, in particular, needed something different from what the criminal courts typically provided. John described his work with young people:

In 1847, I bailed nineteen boys, from seven to fifteen years of age, and in bailing them it was understood, and agreed by the court, that their cases should be continued from term to term for several months, as a season of probation; thus each month at the calling of the docket, I would appear in court, make my report, and thus the cases would pass on for five or six months. At the expiration of this term, twelve of the boys were brought into court at one time, and the scene formed a striking and highly pleasing contrast with their appearance when first arraigned. The judge expressed much pleasure as well as surprise, at their appearance, and remarked, that the object of the law had been accomplished, and expressed his cordial approval of my plan to save and reform. Seven of the number were too poor to pay a fine, although the court fixed the amount at ten cents each, and of course I paid it for them; the parents of the other boys were able to pay the cost, and thus the penalty of the law was answered. The sequel thus far shows, that not one of this number has proved false to the promises of reform they made while on probation. This incident proved conclusively, that this class of boys could be saved from crime and punishment, by the plan which I had marked out, and this was admitted by the judges in both courts.[7]

John was a cobbler, a boot maker, but his inspiration came from helping young people make a better path for themselves. He spent his days around shoes, but he was a reformer, a dreamer. In believing in others, he planted an idea so resilient that it would forever change lives. It changed the state of Massachusetts, which began a statewide salaried probation system after the passing of John Augustus. His dream became the state's dream.

Juvenile Court

Boston, Massachusetts, the home of John Augustus, is believed to have created the first probation department for juveniles in 1878, but the group providing probation services was not associated with any one court. The first juvenile court was created in 1899 in Chicago, Cook County, Illinois, largely because of pressure from women's reform groups. It borrowed two ideas from British reformers: the idea that young people were morally and cognitively different from adults, and the doctrine of *parens patraie*, the state as a parent. The premise was that the state had the right to intervene where parents did not provide proper supervision or adequate care, as in the case of juvenile delinquents.[8]

Prior to the advent of the juvenile court, juveniles and adults were tried in the same courts, and children over the age of seven were kept together with adults in the same facilities. There were eventually attempts to create separate facilities in an effort to protect and rehabilitate young people. These facilities were not only for delinquents, but for the incorrigible (youth who did not generally follow the rules set by parents, schools, or the community), the unsupervised, and orphans.

In Texas, the Juvenile Court Act of 1907, originally House Bill 206, was passed during the thirtieth legislative session. The act provided a separate court for offenders sixteen and under. It also provided for parental notification of arrest and hearings. It stated that "the court may" appoint an attorney for a juvenile, but the judge was not required to notify the accused of counsel. The juvenile could also waive his right to an attorney, in which case the probation officer was required to advocate in the child's best interest.[9]

Juveniles could only be held in the jail preconviction if their appearance at court was a matter of doubt, and they had to be kept in a separate "compartment" from those over the age of sixteen. Essentially, a child could be kept in a cell next to an adult, as long as they were separate cells. If a juvenile was adjudged delinquent, there were three possible dispositions: remain at home, be placed with a suitable family, or be sent to an institution (for boys this was the Gatesville State School for Boys, for girls at the time it was the penitentiary). The maximum commitment for boys was up until their twenty-first birthday. For girls, neither a maximum nor a minimum was prescribed.[10]

This is not the juvenile court we know today or even one that other jurisdictions knew at the time. The Juvenile Court Act of 1907 kept juveniles solely under criminal court jurisdiction and procedural rules—not civil, so the focus remained quite punitive. Nor did criminal jurisdiction and procedure afford separate due process considerations. Despite that, the act of 1907 was a beginning, and later adjustments would make Texas juvenile justice more closely reflect the original dream.

Movement for a separate court for juveniles in Texas began in earnest at least as early as 1902, primarily with the work of the Federation of Women's Clubs, particularly that of the branch in Dallas. Protective legislation for juveniles was drawn up but narrowly defeated in 1905. One of the pioneers of this movement, Sarah Callaway, wrote regularly on the subject for the *Dallas Morning News* under the pen name Pauline Periwinkle. Pauline and the Federation of Women's Clubs were persistent and vocal advocates for the creation and ongoing reform of the juvenile justice system in Texas, as well as throughout the United States.[11]

Why would the cry for reform for young people come from women, and what hope would the movement have in the hands of advocates who had no voting power, and therefore little sway in political matters? Perhaps this was the reason the cry was so resounding, and so persistent. It came from a group that knew very intimately what it was like to be treated as *less*.

Reform: The Cry Started Early

Reformers created the juvenile justice movement, but they have not been able to rest on their laurels. They have continually raised their voices as they notice departures from the original dream or the dilution of the movement's ideals. The Dallas Federation of Women's clubs was the initial advocate of not only the movement, but of its early reforms.

Prior to the creation of juvenile courts, houses of refuge and state training schools were created to provide a separate place for juveniles who were in need of reform. Despite the positive impact of probation as demonstrated by John Augustus, and the mounting evidence favoring community-based efforts today, the call for reform was answered initially by institutions. This had a far-reaching impact on the juvenile justice system.

Property or Priority?

Young people have not always been seen as anything so valuable as our future. Early on, the place occupied by children in society came from another English idea: chattel. The word *chattel* literally means "property." Like the tractor or draft animals in early agricultural society, children served a purpose, but that purpose was to serve the farmer. Children were seen as help in their parents' fields of labor.[12] As society in the Western world rapidly moved from an agricultural to an industrial mode, the role of children in society was much slower to change. The suffrage movement seemed to gain ground first in the area of women's rights and other civil rights for adults. Children were the last bastion in our conception of property. We still claim children as *dependents* on our taxes for a credit, and we have *custody* and are able to fight for custody (that is, control) of children in court.

The movement toward a system in which children were treated differently from adults had trouble gaining traction in a society that failed to fully embrace the logic behind the idea. Reform required more reform in order to move toward the place where children are valued. Despite our current, widespread understanding that people are our greatest resource, and that our future belongs to the young of today, we still struggle with our concepts about the treatment of children. Singing that children are the future is one thing, but the reality is that when children aren't ready to take that place, or don't take their place in society the way society believes they should, there is a hasty recalculation of what is meant when we say that young people are a priority.

Supreme Reform: Does That Make It Good?

Within the first half century of juvenile justice's beginnings, there began to be a struggle over how to keep children separate and protected. Separation and protection—key concepts that make juvenile justice unique—sometimes seem to pull in opposite directions, as if they were mutually exclusive. The concept is that juveniles should be kept apart from adults in a system that is without the rigid formality of procedures for adult offenders. The tradeoff lies in the notion that the juvenile court has the leeway to be lenient with children, even as the children are afforded fewer legal protections than those available to adults. Too often, however, there is no tradeoff, and juveniles are afforded neither leniency nor the protections afforded adults. Without being able to do either effectively, juvenile justice has been woefully inept at remaining distinct from the adult system.

When those within the system and reformers outside the system have been unable to bring about the necessary changes to create distinctions between the treatment of juvenile and adult offenders, it has been left to the judicial system. The justice system, whether it is for adults or children, has always been adversarial in nature. The prosecution attempts to bring the individual to justice, while the defense steps in to protect the individual. The court is designed to interpret, analyze, and bring justice. They are players in the game, but the game has rules, and they are bound to play by those rules. The rules are changed only by the legislative branch, if there is the political will inside and outside the system to bring the change forward. Even so, such change can only happen when the legislative body meets, which is typically too infrequently to have an immediate impact on the overall system, and may only happen when politically expedient. The political arena is also too often adversarial.

The judicial branch has to step in at times. The judicial branch was set up to make sure the players truly play the game within the boundaries of the rules. As a last resort, the judicial branch reluctantly becomes legislative. In this country, the Supreme Court of the United States is the highest court of the land and the interpreter of this and other dreams.

This push and pull between separation and protection of juveniles has been strong, and the Supreme Court has tried to bring these conflicting values into a state of equilibrium. Even for the law of the land, this has been a challenge. This chapter looks at how the keepers of this dream of juvenile justice have attempted to bring about that equilibrium, and the challenges that these landmark cases have brought to the dream.

Kent v. United States: The Worst of Both Worlds?

The early juvenile court envisioned by Judge Mack of Chicago was a relatively informal setting, where all the pomp and circumstance of adult court were avoided as something that a juvenile would not understand. In its purpose, it was probably a good thing for the young person. In the way it was often carried out, however, it could result in carelessness in the process and little or no protection for the young offender.

Morris A. Kent Jr. was a fourteen-year-old male living in the Washington, DC, area when he was arrested for housebreaking and robbery in 1959. The juvenile court placed him on probation. Two years later, in 1961, a woman was robbed and raped by an intruder in her home. Fingerprints taken from the scene were matched with those provided by Kent in the 1959 arrest. Kent was arrested for this crime, questioned, and taken into custody. Kent's case was handled in the District of Columbia Juvenile Court, and was in consideration of waiver from the juvenile system to the adult system. His attorneys requested a hearing on the issue of this waiver, and requested, for the court's full inspection, the social history reports on Kent that were prepared by juvenile probation in 1959. The Juvenile Court of the District of Columbia did not rule on the motions of counsel, however, and after its own "full inspection" of the reports, eventually ordered, without a hearing, the waiver of Kent from juvenile to adult court to face trial. The child and the attorney were not allowed to view the reports from which the decisions were made, and were not allowed a hearing on the decision. There had also been separate psychiatric reports finding that Kent was severely emotionally ill—a finding that might have led authorities to keep the proceedings in juvenile court. Instead, Kent was sent to adult court, was found guilty, and was given a sentence of thirty to ninety years.[13]

The attorneys challenged the validity and legality of a waiver based on no hearing, and on information that was essentially kept from the view of the attorneys and their client. Upon appeal, the court of appeals affirmed the original court's process as valid. It was then appealed to the US Supreme Court.

In 1966, the US Supreme Court agreed to hear Kent's case. According to the American Bar Association's (ABA) Public Education Division, in a majority opinion authored by Justice Abe Fortas, a noted proponent of children's rights, the court "ruled that Kent was entitled to a hearing and to a statement of the reasons for the juvenile court's decision to waive jurisdiction. In its opinion, the majority also expressed concerns that the juvenile courts were not living up to their promise. In fact, the majority speculated that there may be grounds for concern that the child receives the worst of both worlds [in juvenile court]: that he gets neither the protections accorded to adults nor the solicitous care and regenerative treatment postulated for children." A particular concern was whether juvenile courts had received the resources, personnel, and facilities they needed to adequately serve youth charged with violations of the law.[14]

In re Gault: Blurred Lines

Advocates within the juvenile justice system began struggling to develop a basis for keeping juvenile cases separate from the beginning. Most judges involved had pursued their careers in adult courts, before juvenile courts were established. Even after the creation of a separate court, most judges did juvenile work on a part-time basis, with adult proceedings occupying most of their time, just as adult cases monopolized the community's attention and political will.

This continued through the first seven decades after the creation of the juvenile court and remained unchallenged until a questionable phone call was made by fifteen-year-old Gerald Gault. With little previous record to speak of (he was in the company of another youth when the latter stole a woman's wallet), Gault allegedly made a very adolescent and obscene phone call to a neighbor. Once police learned of the call, the boy was arrested and taken into custody; Gault's parents only learned of this through a friend who had seen him arrested. In a defense claimed by juveniles before and since, Gault maintained that a friend of his, another juvenile, actually made the call from his home and was the one who used vulgar language.[15]

Gerald was soon in front of a judge for what juvenile justice at that time called a hearing. He was not warned of the possible consequences of his actions, and no witnesses were presented. He was asked questions without protections against self-incrimination, and no attorney represented him (At the time of the Gault decision, many judges in the United States were not lawyers.) Gault was found delinquent and was ordered to a state training school for what amounted to six years, up to his twenty-first birthday. Had he been an adult, he would have faced a maximum of two months in jail and a five- to fifty-dollar fine.

He was released after the appeal. Gault has since indicated that the facility he was sent to, which was charged with his rehabilitation, did little other than warehouse him for that time.[16]

Without those inside or outside the system being able to act, this case made its way to the United States Supreme Court Justices in 1967, and the case was overturned. The Supreme Court, in an eight-to-one decision, indicated that while juveniles were to be treated separately, they should be afforded the same due process as adults in matters where liberty was at stake. While a logical and widely heralded decision, it forever changed the way juvenile courts operated. The decision challenged the very balance described some sixty years earlier by Judge Mack of Chicago. The justices in the Gault case basically denounced the idea of *parens patraie*, indicating that regardless of the benevolence that the juvenile court offers, its wide discretion is a poor substitute for due process.[17]

Again from the ABA Public Education Division, "The Supreme Court's decision in *Gault* was not unanimous. In a dissent, Justice Potter Stewart warned that by requiring many of the same due process guarantees in juvenile cases that are required in criminal cases, the court was converting juvenile proceedings into criminal proceedings." In doing so, he argued, the court was missing an important distinction. The object of juvenile proceedings was the "correction of a condition." The proceedings were not intended to be adversarial. Juvenile courts functioned as public social agencies striving to find the right solution to the problem of juvenile delinquency. The object of criminal courts, in contrast, was conviction and punishment of those who commit wrongful acts. Justice Stewart noted that in the nineteenth century, before juvenile courts were established, juveniles tried in criminal courts were given the same due process as adults. They were, in like manner, subject to the harshest of punishments for their crimes, including the death penalty. Juvenile courts were not perfect, Justice Stewart agreed, stating that "in many areas the performance of these agencies has fallen disappointingly short of the hopes and dreams of the courageous pioneers who first conceived them." But by blurring the distinction between juvenile proceedings and criminal proceedings, the court was inviting "a long step backwards into the nineteenth century."[18]

In re Winship: **The End of Benevolence?**
Samuel Winship was a twelve-year-old young man charged with

theft for taking $112 from a woman's pocketbook that was in a locker. He was found delinquent by a preponderance of the evidence, and sentenced to a state school for a minimum of eighteen months, with annual extensions possible up until his eighteenth birthday—some six years later. His attorneys appealed the burden of proof.[19]

In 1970, the Supreme Court agreed with the attorney that the preponderance of evidence standard for delinquency cases was insufficient. Preponderance of the evidence has been described by some as just over fifty percent, and is the standard of proof in civil litigation. Winship's case moved the burden of proof in juvenile cases from preponderance of the evidence to the adult criminal standard of "beyond a reasonable doubt."[20]

Chief Justice Warren Burger dissented from the majority opinion in *Winship*, joined by Justice Potter Stewart. By moving the juvenile courts closer to procedures used in the criminal trials of adults, the dissenters argued, the court was also moving away from the original idea of juvenile courts as benevolent and less formal institutions equipped to deal flexibly with the unique needs of juvenile offenders. From the Winship decision, "I cannot regard it as a manifestation of progress," Chief Justice Burger asserted, "to transform juvenile courts into criminal courts, which is what we are well on the way to accomplishing."[21]

Clearly, reforms brought by the US Supreme Court have in many ways resulted in a better version of the court system for juveniles. The protections provided by the outcome of cases like *Gault*, *Winship*, *Kent*, and others protect against the abuse of children. This is a very positive outcome. In making these changes, however, as the dissenters have pointed out every step of the way, the informality and non-adversarial nature dreamed up by the inventors of the juvenile court process continue to give ground to the adversarial nature of the adult court system. An adversarial system, by nature, does not work in the best interest of the juvenile. An adversarial system is not based on the belief that a child is malleable and able to change. Some critics claim the solution lies in making the distinction between juvenile and adult justice apply only to the punishment phase. This approach suggests that a court can flip on and off its underlying philosophy when dealing with an adult or a juvenile, or between the trial and the disposition. Even now, the punishment phase determined by juvenile courts has not always been so distinct, with correctional institutions that resemble adult prisons and a growing list of offenses and situations that can have a juvenile case transferred to the adult court.

Due Process Redux—the Texas Landmark: *Morales v. Turman*

Despite the findings in early Supreme Court cases, much of the time the juvenile court system continued its usual practices. In 1971, the Supreme Court of Texas had to deal with due process issues some four short years following the *Gault* decision. It started with a fifteen-year-old girl.

Alicia Morales was the oldest of eight children and, at fifteen, was forced to work and provide her paycheck to her father. She argued that she should be able to keep the money she had earned, and her father responded by having her committed to the Texas Youth Commission (TYC) through the El Paso juvenile court, for disobedience. Her being turned over to the state's care amounted to an agreed judgment by the parents to send their child away to a state institution. Due process was less than an afterthought; no notice of charges, no court appearance, and no representation. At some point after her commitment, Alicia sought representation, and the federal court lawsuit, *Morales v. Turman*, was filed in 1971.

According to an online brief history of Texas juvenile justice, "Upon hearing the appeal, Judge William Wayne Justice sent a letter to all 2,500 TYC youth then in custody asking them whether they had received a court hearing and an attorney before being sent to TYC. Most said they had had a hearing, but over a third had not been represented by counsel. The state agreed to a declaratory judgment that gave the Texas Legislature time, during its next session in 1973, to reconsider the bill it had defeated the previous session—a bill that had incorporated the due process rights the Supreme Court had mandated in the 1967 *Gault* decision. The bill was enacted as Title 3 of the Texas Family Code in the 1973 session."[22]

In 1972, Judge Justice granted the motion for an opportunity to interview every youth confined in TYC with the assistance of law students from the University of Texas and Southern Methodist University. These interviews caused the plaintiffs to shift their focus on what they viewed to be the constitutional right of incarcerated juveniles to receive medical and psychiatric treatment. This focus moved it from an issue that wasn't addressed in Texas statutes toward a constitutionally protected issue. In other words, it gave the case legs. The case drew national attention. The plaintiffs' original two attorneys were joined by five from the Civil Rights Division of the US Department of Justice and two from the Mental Health Law Project, a public-interest law firm that specialized in the rights of institutionalized persons.[23]

This is the description of the courtroom testimony according to the brief history of Texas juvenile justice article: "The testimony at the six-week trial in the summer of 1973 revealed that 60 percent of the boys were there for stealing, 19 percent for disobedience and immoral conduct, and only 9 percent for crimes of violence. Of the large number of girls then in TYC (housed at the training schools in Brownwood, Gainesville, and Crockett), 68 percent were committed for disobedience or immoral conduct and 4 percent for crimes of violence."[24]

In a monumental decision, the judge ruled that a "number of practices at Texas Youth Council facilities constituted cruel and unusual punishment that violated the Eighth Amendment to the United States Constitution." Examples of these practices included, according to Shaw & Penn (2001), "staff members routinely and unnecessarily punishing youth through beatings, solitary confinement, the use of chemical crowd-control devices, and the utilization of drugs instead of psychotherapy as a means of controlling behavior. Judge Justice also concluded that the school's staff failed to protect the inmates from violence and personal injury and that most employees lacked proper qualifications and training for supervising troubled youths."[25]

"After years of negotiations and various court proceedings rising to the US Supreme Court, a settlement agreement was reached in 1984 and a monitoring committee finished its work in 1988—seventeen years after the case was filed. The Court of Appeals rejected the plaintiff's assertion of a constitutional right to treatment for incarcerated juveniles. Nonetheless, the Morales case established the first national standards for juvenile justice and corrections," according to a brief history of Texas juvenile justice.[26]

In Texas, it prompted a number of changes, including the prohibition of corporal punishment, extended periods of isolation, and all forms of inhumane treatment. The decision also required the establishment of an effective youth grievance and mistreatment investigation system; minimum staff qualification and training requirements; individualized, specialized, and community-based treatment programs; TYC-operated halfway-house programs; and a county assistance program to help reduce commitments to TYC by providing state funds for probation services for youth in their local communities—a commitment to community-based options.[27]

The Morales case set the standard for juvenile facility treatment, but as the recent Texas Youth Commission scandals show, history can repeat itself. Many of the same protections and safeguards clearly identified by this case and others are flaunted in practice today. The situation begs correction.

Protecting the Ship

The idea of rehabilitation is one of the hallmark features that distinguish the juvenile system from its adult counterpart. In the United States this has been particularly difficult. Historically, the United States has taken an extreme stance in approaching the problem of crime in our communities. Protection of the accused individual consistently takes a distant second place to questions of public safety. Criminals are separated from the community by incarcerating them. In other words, punishment is king, and Texas always seems to want to do everything bigger. According to the Pew report of 2008, "The number of prisoners in California dropped by 4,000 last year, making Texas's prison system the nation's largest, at about 172,000."[28] Texas had increased the total number of incarcerated to 218,000 in 2016, but had dropped its incarceration rate, and now has the seventh largest rate in the nation. [29]

Rehabilitation (rather than punishment) is the idea that the person involved in criminal activity can be restored to his or her rightful place in the community. In juvenile justice, too often, the models for rehabilitation and punishment seem indistinguishable. The conundrum might lie in the fact that institutional reform preceded the idea of rehabilitation, meaning that the correctional institutions were the first attempted solution. The pendulum from punishment to rehabilitation swings back and forth, but never fully toward rehabilitation.

The national movement for juvenile corrections started in the 1820s, and the state training schools in juvenile justice were built before the juvenile court systems took hold. Instead of one supplanting the other in the juvenile system, the community-based probation side has often seemed built to serve the correctional side. There has been the recognition in society that some should not be in the community, and that the system for community rehabilitation is woefully inadequate in size and scope. While a solution seems evident—push available resources to the community-based side—it has remained out of reach.[30]

In Texas, the first state school, at the time known as a house of correction, was built in Gatesville in 1889, ten years before the Chicago juvenile court was established. Texas's state school also came about as a result of the work of women reformers. The Texas Woman's Christian Temperance Union (WCTU) members visited the Rusk Penitentiary in 1886 and noticed there were young children and adults housed together in the same environment. Upset by what they observed, they lobbied for legislation and for voters to get upset as well.[31] According to *The Handbook of Texas* online, the WCTU was established "to promote total abstinence from alcoholic beverages and to put liquor dealers out of business for the purpose of reducing crime, poverty, and immorality. Temperance women, however, followed the lead of national president Frances Willard in using the organization to structure a public and political role for women." The focus "on the drinking man's neglect and abuse of his wife and children" and speaking as "organized motherhood," the WCTU promoted an agenda of social-welfare reforms and asked for women's suffrage in the name of "home protection."[32] Membership was around fifteen hundred in 1887, and dropped to fewer than six hundred after the group's endorsement of suffrage. Membership did not rebound until the 1890s.[33]

The Handbook of Texas online also provides the history of North Texas's leader of the WCTU, Jenny Bland Beauchamp. Beauchamp(1833-1914), a temperance reformer and writer, was the second president of the Woman's Christian Temperance Union in Texas. Mrs. Beauchamp "was a resident of Denton, Texas and the wife of Rev. Sylvester Allen Beauchamp, a Baptist minister. They had six children. Mrs. Beauchamp had no previous leadership experience when she took over as president of the WCTU in 1883."[34] She had been described as a quiet woman who liked to read and take care of her children. Despite meager travel funds, she organized local unions in more than twenty Texas counties during the four years that she held office. Given Jenny's leadership defending families from the impact of alcohol, it is not surprising that the temperance group also focused on the welfare of children and other problems for children in society. Beauchamp also led the temperance movement in organizing a rescue home in Fort Worth for girls. Jenny Beauchamp began "the WCTU tradition of petitioning the state legislature for specific social reforms, and under her administration the organization lobbied successfully for a state orphanage at Corsicana in 1887."[35] In 1886, Jenny was among those members of the WCTU who visited the Rusk Penitentiary. During that visit, she was taken on a tour by the local chaplain, who pointed out that around 10 percent of the residents (three hundred out of three thousand) were under the age of sixteen.

The chaplain informed his visitor that they should really be in separate quarters, and his visitor was obviously listening. Mrs. Beauchamp launched a petition drive to have juvenile inmates separated from adult criminals. The legislation creating separate facilities passed in 1887. What started as a simple visit led to the legislature authorizing a house of correction for juveniles, the Gatesville State School for Boys.[36]

Gatesville sits in central Texas in Coryell County. It was basically farmland in the nineteenth century, and seven hundred acres were purchased to be used for a house of correction for juveniles. In the beginning, this was an all-male facility. The site was described by a state commissioner as land that "commands the most picturesque and beautiful scenery we have ever had the pleasure of witnessing," and the buildings were described as "imposing [in] appearance and pleasing to the eye." The school of reform was meant to be different from the adult institutions and was solely for youth. Despite such pleasantries, this was unmistakably an institution. The guards had experience in adult institutions; they carried batons, rode on horseback, and employed dogs, and corporal punishment was what constituted correction for behavior.[37]

The new institution was launched with unbridled optimism for something new, something better. In addition to being the first of its kind in Texas, it was essentially the first of its kind in the South, and was followed by many others. Early on, the programming was modeled on farm labor: the inmates worked both inside the walls of the school and as contract labor for nearby farmers. Education was an element, but not in the spring or fall—those were farming and harvesting times.

Eighty-six young people were transported from the prison system to become the first occupants, and over half of them—forty-six—were African American. While this book is not about that topic, it is impossible to talk about the history of juvenile justice without recognizing the disproportionate minority contact within the criminal and juvenile justice systems, and this was evident early in Texas. Despite early warning signs, the new dawn of juvenile justice had almost all sides excited. It is reported there was even a footrace among two of the young men on that first day, to see who would be the first resident of this new experiment in justice.[38]

Further reforms began early, partly because of concerns about the ways the school resembled a prison in its appearance and procedures. In 1913, new juvenile justice legislation was passed, in large measure to create guidelines for the Gatesville State School for Boys. The crafters of this legislation envisioned a more scientific approach that would stress education over labor in the effort to reform young men. This approach gained ground in 1913 under the leadership of A. W. Eddins, then superintendent of Gatesville, and again in 1916, after the creation of a girls school in Gainesville, Texas, under the leadership of Carrie Weaver Smith. But the political climate soon changed, and after the departure of these leaders things regressed.[39]

By the 1920s, the focus on educational and vocational rehabilitation started by these two leaders had declined significantly, and the use of labor and military regimentation increased. By the 1940s, reform again seemed imminent. The Texas State Board of Control (TBC) fired the superintendents of the state schools on September 1, 1941, after a new round of abuse scandals at the facilities. Audits of the two state schools resulted in a report portraying the schools as "little more than prisons,"according to Bush (2010).[40]

The TBC hired Robert Winship, of Junction, Texas, to bring about needed reforms in the schools. Winship felt the schools should be places of last resort, and not the first stop for young people. He lamented that only sixteen counties provided real probation services in Texas, and argued that the communities needed to step up their services. In an interview with the *Fort Worth Star-Telegram*, Winship explained his general philosophy:

> We do not regard the boys here as having committed crimes. They are, rather, delinquent boys who are in need of guardianship above and beyond what they are getting at home. This means that instead of their being punished like adults, they are regarded as being children and not fully responsible for what they do. They are somewhat like a boy who is sick. Such a boy has something wrong with him physically, but these boys have something wrong with them because they are sick socially, and need help where the proper guidance in the community has failed.[41]

While his ideas of reform had been publicly lauded, those in charge inside the walls of the school offered resistance to these changes, as they had from the beginning and would throughout the school's history. It seemed that anytime a leader attempted to bring about a concrete shift in philosophy or practice, the guards at the juvenile facilities reminded that leader where the real power rested. The juvenile guards, in essence, allowed chaos to ensue inside the walls and allowed young men to escape into the towns to help sway the sentiment of the community. Winship lasted in the post less than two years, and the efforts at reform once again gave way to a system of control and enforcement.

In the summer of 1948, Texas consulted with Richard Clenenden, the consultant on training schools for the US Children's Bureau, and a national expert on juvenile delinquency and juvenile justice. He suggested a major overhaul was in order to change the direction of the state schools, and offered some of the following suggestions: smaller institutions in the form of group homes with 50 to 150 children; less rural locations; and the inclusion of families as part of the treatment. It is haunting how these words have echoed hollow through most of the juvenile correctional system for the past sixty years.[42]

During this time, the Texas State Training School Code Commission began a study of the schools. A 1948 survey sponsored by the commission found that over half of Gatesville's inmates had been previous residents of the school, with almost two-thirds of adult prisoners describing themselves as "graduates" of Gatesville.[43] Texas Governor Beauford H. Jester and the Texas Training School Code Commission held a press conference in Austin on February 6, 1949, that had been eagerly anticipated. After eighteen months of study, the commission wrote a bill that "proposed to go far beyond its original mandate to repair the state's broken juvenile training schools." With great fanfare, they announced plans for "the most extensive youth program ever developed" in Texas—or in the nation.[44]

Bush (2010) describes the intent of the legislation:

> The commission's legislation proposed to fix the system's sizeable problems by placing all state and local juvenile justice agencies under the supervision of the Texas State Youth Development Council. The new agency would function within existing state departments until 1957, when it would be reorganized as a stand-alone agency, the Texas Youth Council (TYC). TYC was charged with devising diagnostic, classification, and treatment programs based on child psychology rather than penology. Each child was to be sent to a single diagnostic center where an intake team of trained professionals would formulate a rehabilitation plan based on psychiatric interview and observation, a battery of psychological and intelligence tests, and a life history provided

by local authorities. From there, the child might be placed in any number of facilities that were to be constructed in the following few years. Ideally, the diagnostic center would have the option of sending juveniles to community-based programs run locally. Thus, TYC's other key task was to assist local governments in organizing diversion programs, with the stated goals being a sharp reduction in the population of existing training schools and an expansion in the overall number of facilities for delinquent youth. Although completely phasing out Gatesville and Gainesville was never seriously considered, those institutions were expected to jettison "the whole correctional system and philosophy" of mass custody and control.[45]

While the talk of change seemed like an appropriate response to Clenenden's recommendations, it largely remained talk.

Given singular authority throughout the state and staffed with trained experts and professionals, TYC promised to wipe clean the persistent abuses of the past and start over with modern approaches to delinquency.

Driven by unprecedented optimism and energy, TYC seemed, to many observers, to be a step in the right direction to move beyond the turbulent history of juvenile justice in Texas. The training-school system, however, proved deeply entrenched, as was the belief that most juvenile offenders were simply criminals who neither deserved nor could benefit from the protective umbrella of rehabilitative services. The tension between the models of juvenile rehabilitation and adult punishment that had dominated the previous half century and would not likely be resolved quickly, if at all.[46]

By the early 1960s, the optimism of the previous decade had waned. The hopes of restructuring and using science to transform the institutions of Texas were products of wishful thinking. The state agency's new name appeared to be like thinly applied varnish on a battered antique. While the varnish looked nice in the beginning, it wasn't long before the cracks began to show. TYC came under intense scrutiny as allegations of abuse continued. No action was taken from the inside, and outsiders seemed either unable or unwilling to intervene—until *Morales v. Turman*, in the early 1970s. The rulings in that case shook TYC to its core, eventually sounding a death knell to the Gatesville

State School. As a reform school, Gatesville was an apparent waste of time, effort, and resources; worse, it put young people in harm's way for almost one hundred years.[47]

Morales prompted major reforms to the existing institutions, bringing needed and sweeping changes. But by the 1990s with increasing public and legislative demands to "get tough" on juvenile offenders, and particularly with the Texas legislative session of 1995, TYC again leaned heavily on its old practices. With an ever-increasing population, the reliance on secure, prison-like settings erased much of the progress of the reforms. Highly publicized abuse scandals at two of the institutions in the early 2000s, however—sexual abuse allegations by administrators at facilities in Pyote, Texas, and at the Ron Jackson State School in Brownwood, Texas—played a central role in attracting further national scrutiny. In 2007 the legislative body again got involved by passing Senate Bill 103, which drastically reduced the population from over five thousand inmates in 2006 to roughly one thousand today. With such a reduction, it seemed that things would change, but advocacy groups on the outside continued to place TYC under a microscope. In 2009, the Texas Sunset Commission, the state body that examines whether or not an agency is functioning as intended, recommended the abolishment of TYC, but legislators granted a temporary reprieve with the stipulation that quick headway be made with reforms. The Sunset Commission was charged with continuing its study and making a report in the 82nd session in 2011.[48]

It is rather easy to look at historical examples of failure and feel that education and evidence could help our system change. But recent headlines indicate this is not a history from which we have wisely learned. In 2009, two judges from Luzerne County, Pennsylvania, Judge Mark A. Ciavarella Jr. and former Senior Judge Michael T. Conahan, were accused of taking $2.6 million for sending children to two facilities owned by a Pittsburgh businessman. It is an extreme example, but it is emblematic of an endemic problem—the courts serving institutions.[49]

Closer to home, the 82nd legislative session ended on May 31, 2011, and what was known as SB 653, signed into law by Governor Rick Perry, merged the Texas Juvenile Probation Commission with the institutional system. After being independent for a short thirty years—with positive results for probation and not-so-positive results for institutions—the two systems are now under a single agency. The Texas Juvenile Probation Commission was formed in 1981, in part because of concern that the system focused on institutions, and in part as a result of the findings in *Morales v. Turman*. The commission was a separate organization with an emphasis on probation, properly trained probation officers, and community-based services. Under SB 653, the new system puts an end to that separate emphasis and leaves the probation and institution sides to negotiate for limited resources. Since 2007, the number of institutions has been reduced from thirteen to five, but these moves have resulted primarily in cost savings and not a redistribution of resources to the probation side of juvenile justice.[50]

Is history bound to repeat itself, or is it something we can learn from? We like to think that we can recognize the mistakes of the past and avoid repeating them. The twenty-first-century movement toward evidence-based practices—utilizing research to determine the programs and responses that are truly effective for young people—offers promise, but it may be too early to tell if the idea of what works can hold firm in the face of a pendulum of political will that historically swings in favor of institutions.

TWO

Juvenile Justice History: Tarrant County

Tarrant County is likely not unique in having many services for children, but it started early and shared some aspects of the dream for a reformed juvenile system. In 1887, with the railroads furthering the expansion westward, one train brought unexpected cargo to Fort Worth. Children from the Northeast who had been abandoned were loaded up and sent west as part of a social experiment known as the "orphan train movement." These were the "leftovers," for the stronger kids had already been taken off the trains to work in farms or factories.[51] Methodist missionary minister I. Z. T. Morris took these children in and, working with local residents and the railroad, helped them find homes. This was the beginning of the Children's Home Society, chartered in 1904 as the Texas Children's Home and Aid Society. While orphaned children were sometimes difficult to place, unwed mothers faced a greater stigma and found few services to assist them. That began to change in Texas and in the nation in large part due to the work and service of Edna Gladney.[52]

Edna Gladney worked as the superintendent of the Texas Children's Home and Aid Society for thirty-three years. The society's name was later changed to the Gladney Center for Adoption in honor of this woman. Gladney worked tirelessly in her efforts to look out for children who couldn't look out for themselves. This was demonstrated both in the way she cared for kids with whom she had direct contact and also in the way she championed legislation. She led two major fights for change in adoption practices: first in removing the stigma of illegitimacy from birth records (the first state in the Southwest to do so), and also in giving adopted children the same inheritance rights as biological children. Under its original name, the Gladney Center was Texas's first agency to provide services for unwed mothers and adoptive homes for children.[53]

Lena Holston Pope was another pioneer. She opened the Lena Pope Home in Fort Worth in the early 1900s to help young children who needed a home. Mrs. Pope had such a compelling vision that she attracted the most influential men in Fort Worth to her cause, including William Monnig (owner of one of the most important early department stores in Texas), John Marvin Leonard (one of the Leonard brothers—the dominant retailers in early Fort Worth), C. A. Lupton (president of Coca-Cola distribution in Fort Worth), and Amon G. Carter (publisher and founder of the *Fort Worth Star-Telegram*). Under the vision and leadership of Lena Pope, care for children in Tarrant County became a community priority.[54]

In 1915, the Women's Cooperative Home was chartered, with the charge of taking in destitute women and children. The home later expanded to provide care for women and children whose husbands and fathers were training at Camp Bowie. The organization was later renamed the All Church Home for Children, currently ACH Child and Family Services.[55]

Under the leadership of these agencies, it is not surprising that Fort Worth and Tarrant County became a haven for underserved and at-risk children. For more than a century, the population has provided the compassion, ingenuity, and innovation that have allowed Tarrant County Juvenile Services and the community to positively influence the field of juvenile justice and children's services beyond the borders of the county and the state.

Tarrant County Juvenile Court, now known as Tarrant County Juvenile Services, began with an unfunded mandate passed by the legislative session in 1907. The law creating the court was passed without any measures to support local jurisdictions. The act specifically stated that a probation officer could be appointed, but that he would serve without compensation. If appointed, the probation officer would be notified of arrests and hearings, investigate cases, be present at hearings, represent the interests of the child, furnish the court with information as requested, and take charge of the juvenile before and after court. The officer would be allowed visitation, would enforce the court's orders, and would perform other such services as ordered by the court.[56]

The Tarrant County Juvenile Court is believed to be the very first operational juvenile court in Texas. It was the beginning of a series of pioneering initiatives taken by the county. In 1906, a year before the state took legislative action, I. Z. T. Morris and others began meeting in Fort Worth to determine how to deal with the issue of juvenile delinquents in the county and to discuss supporting legislation for a possible juvenile court. Reverend Morris had argued against a separate court in 1904 but began to see its potential value.[57] The county, without funding, started what would be another hallmark of the court—partnership. Tarrant County was working with the Young Men's Christian Association (YMCA) of Fort Worth in planning a juvenile court in early March 1907—before the Juvenile Court Act had passed legislation, which happened on April 5, 1907. It became effective ninety days later, on July 5, 1907. Chief James Maddox of the Fort Worth Police Department also spent time in Austin lobbying for a juvenile court.[58]

On July 2, 1907, the county, the police department, the YMCA, and United Charities agreed to bring juveniles picked up by the police to the boys division of the YMCA, at the time led by R. P. Smith. The secretary of the boys division, Mr. E. B. Travis, began what was called the "probation hour" on Sunday evenings. Young men placed in his charge appeared and reported on what they were doing to stay on the straight and narrow (as they were required to do). In one of the initial reports, according to the *Fort Worth Star-Telegram*, things seemed to be going well: "Each of the boys gave a detailed account of his actions during the past week, which was not only satisfactory to Mr. Travis but showed that the boys were appreciating their probation by living correct lives."[59]

Despite its informal status, the court was recognized early among peers for its effectiveness. In a county judges' meeting in Dallas in February 1908, the Dallas Federation of Women's Clubs had the following to report about Tarrant County Juvenile Court, its probation officer, E. B. Travis, and Judge John Terrell, according to the *Dallas Morning News*:

> The greatest efficiency in juvenile court work was shown by Tarrant County, where the commissioners have voluntarily provided for a paid probationary officer. Judge Terrell of Fort Worth and his probationary officer Mr. Travis were present and showed how effective the work had become where properly enforced. They have perfected a card system of probational reports, arranged much after the card system used in the public libraries, whereby at a moment's notice the entire history of the delinquent and his appearances in court can be traced.

Mr. Travis, who plays a sort of Big Brother part to Fort Worth delinquents, exhibited a number of savings bank books he had taken out in the names of boys for whom he had found jobs, or boys who were already at work, but who were spending their money in bad ways. The boys bring him their wages regularly, he banks it, and they can only check it out by his countersigning the check. In this way, he supervises their expenditures and encourages thrift. Some of the balances showed $20 to $50 after legitimate expenses had been defrayed. Thus practical training in business had resulted in several other boys coming into court and voluntarily submitting to probation supervision, so that they could save money too.[60]

The Tarrant County Juvenile Court would officially become the Court of Tarrant County on August 14, 1908, after county commissioners initially balked and almost lost the court's probation officer to rival Dallas County. It is on this date in August that the Commissioner's Court of Tarrant County finally authorized the juvenile court, and began to employ an officer, E. B. Travis, at the salary of $75 per month.[61]

In early August 1908, County Judge John Terrell offered an early glimpse of the philosophy that would continue to guide the court: In reply to a letter from the Dallas Federation of Women's Clubs asking for a statement of his position in regard to the juvenile court law, Judge Terrell wrote the following letter published in the *Fort Worth Star-Telegram*:

Mrs. A. H. McCarty, Mrs. J. J. Jarvis, Mrs. N. B. Davis Committee, City:

Dear Madams—Answering your favor of the 13th inst.—requesting an expression from me upon juvenile court matters. I take pleasure in stating my views upon this, to me, most vital subject.

The club women of Texas were largely instrumental in the passage of this law, and in my judgement no legislative enactment of recent years will prove so beneficent, where properly enforced. Unless the officers have an interest in the work, unless they believe there is so much good in the worst of us, the law is useless. But to the probation officer or Judge who realizes that in the erring boy before him are the sturdy elements which go to the making of the useful citizen of tomorrow, and will always keep in mind that this boy along with your boy will in a few years shape the destiny of this republic, the opportunity is presented of doing a great and patriotic work. . . .

I thoroughly believe in the probative system of dealing with erring boys. In many cases suspended judgement is necessary, and the boy put upon probation, pending good behavior. But merely to let him go accomplishes little good. His environment must be investigated; he must be made to feel that some one has an interest in his welfare. On this account, I am in favor of a law giving us paid probation officers. As a matter of economy, it is cheaper to save the boy than to punish the criminal.

I favor a state home or homes for delinquents and failing in this, a training school in large counties like Tarrant County. We must have some place where we can put the boy upon whom the probative system fails. The county road is the worst place that can be imagined for a boy, but in extreme cases we have to do this—but only when all other methods have failed.

I could cite numerous instances of boys who before they came into the juvenile court, were continually brought up for theft and burglary, who are now holding good positions and honored by those who know them. The percentage of youthful offenders who can really be called "incorrigible" is small, and there is some way to reach the heart and pride of every boy.

Of the 200 boys we have had in the juvenile court, only 15 have come back charged with another offense. Only four boys have come back the third time.

In almost all cases of boys before us, the fault is not in the boy himself, but in the lack of home influence. The boy is not to blame. All he needs is a chance. And I shall always give him that chance, or as many chances as I can when he is trying to make a man of himself.

Whenever I can be of service in procuring needed legislation to broaden the scope of the juvenile laws, or in the securing of a state or county detention home for delinquents, command me.

Respectfully, John L. Terrell [62]

Being proactive, unique, innovative, and a model were early trademarks of the Tarrant County Juvenile Court, but such is the history with many budding juvenile courts. The real test, as noted in the history of juvenile justice itself, is not the start but the journey and the sustainability of such efforts.

THREE

The Foundation: Building Something Worthwhile

There were six chief probation officers in the first forty years of the juvenile court's existence. By all accounts, these were fine men who offered great leadership and direction to the court. They were the foundation of the court. Much of what can be learned about some of these early leaders appears in newspaper articles and old case files.

E. B. Travis—Promising but Brief Beginnings

E. B. Travis offered early leadership of the court and, by all accounts, led well with the backing of Judge John Terrell. John Terrell advocated for the work of juvenile courts in general, throughout Texas and beyond. In the early days of the court, prominent juvenile court Judge Ben Lindsey of Denver, Colorado—another early model court—and the "father of juvenile court," the Reverend Dr. A. S. Orne of Chicago, visited Fort Worth to speak about the dream of juvenile justice. Orne had been the earliest and most vocal advocate to bring about a juvenile court in Chicago, and he continued his advocacy in twenty-eight other states.[63]

Mr. Travis initially held a "probation hour" on Sunday evenings with the young men on his caseload reporting in to him and to each other about what they were doing to change. In some of the more serious cases, adolescents were required to work county road duty with adult offenders. This was hard labor.[64] Travis helped young people in several ways, including training and helping them to open bank accounts to save money. Having such a way with young people, he even led some boys not on probation to voluntarily submit to supervision. As one older brother put it, "Do you think I'm going to stand for me kid brother having twenty dollars in the bank and me not have a cent?"[65]

Travis and Judge Terrell continually worked toward community partnerships and did so in an effort to find juveniles appropriate employment. One such partnership was with the Armour meatpacking plant. The Armour plant agreed to give employment to "certain classes of boys" on probation. Judge Terrell praised the employees of the plant in the *Dallas Morning News*, stating that they "manifested great interest in the juvenile problem, and I think in this way we will be able to make many good men of boys that would have otherwise been criminals, perhaps."[66]

Travis worked initially as an employee of the YMCA as the secretary of the boys division. The YMCA partnered with the court prior to the passage of the Texas Juvenile Court Act. In an early August 1908 meeting of the Commissioner's Court, an agenda item included the payment of the probation officer. The commissioners did not agree to the request, and it quickly led to Mr. Travis rethinking his post. In an article in the *Dallas Morning News* the same day, a headline read, "E. B. Travis leaves for Dallas." The very group that had praised his work in February, the Dallas Federation of Women's Clubs, had agreed to pay his salary in Dallas County.[67]

Two days later, the Commissioner's Court reconvened at the request of Judge John Terrell and authorized a subsidy for Travis's YMCA salary. The YMCA had been paying Travis $25 per month, and the county officially employed their first probation officer by paying him another $75 per month. The move seemed to settle this bit of rivalry between the neighboring counties and offered stability to Mr. Travis, the court, and the young delinquents within the county.[68] Signs of rivalry from Dallas didn't take too long to rekindle, however; Dallas County hired its own man a few days later, with the local paper suggesting that this man was the county's choice over Travis all along.[69]

Politics continued to interfere. In late December 1910, all the work of the court came to an abrupt halt as the Commissioner's Court, without discussion or explanation, voted to cease paying Travis's salary. A *Dallas Morning News* headline stated the matter in four short words: "Tarrant Juvenile Court Abolished." At the time, Travis had been assisted by four volunteers, but Judge Terrell insisted that the court's work required the full-time services of at least one person. Various advocates lobbied for the position to be filled even if Travis wasn't reappointed. One of the advocates suggested that the county might not want to reappoint him since Travis was not born in Texas. By midyear 1911, the matter had not been resolved; Travis accepted another post, and applications were being considered for the Tarrant County position. Among those submitted was an application from a woman which made headlines but did not receive a positive response from the commissioners, who insisted they were willing to begin services again if they could "find the right man" for the job.[70]

S. J. (Sam) Callaway—The Fresh Restart

Despite claims by Tarrant County that they were ready to begin services again, it wasn't until 1913 that legislation breathed life back into the idea of a juvenile court in Tarrant County. This session mandated at least two officers.

The law in 1913 required any county with a population of more than 100,000 to employ (not just to appoint, but to pay) two probation officers to handle juvenile matters. The chief officer could be paid up to $1,500 per month, with the second officer making up to $900. The county could also hire an attendance officer to work in the probation office to deal with the newly created compulsory school-attendance laws. The probation officer was to be a discreet person of good moral character. He was to take an oath and be given all the powers of a police officer or sheriff, including powers of arrest. The law became effective July 1, 1913, some eighteen months after Tarrant County had abruptly halted Travis's work. For County Judge Jesse Brown, the search to revive the dream began in earnest in May.[71]

A May 1913 article in the *Fort Worth Star-Telegram* reported that the eighteen-month hiatus in the work of the juvenile court had not curtailed interest in the project. The article stated an overwhelming response—more than nine hundred applications—had been received for the two available positions. The act of 1913 required that the county school superintendent and other superintendents of schools within the county make nominations to the county judge. County Superintendent S. J. Callaway received the applications in order to make a recommendation to Judge Jesse M. Brown. Another *Fort Worth Star-Telegram* article in June of 1913 indicated the county superintendent and representatives from each major district—Fort Worth ISD and Arlington ISD—would narrow the field for Judge Brown, giving him two recommendations apiece—up to a total of six names.[72]

But on July 1, 1913, in a letter to the Commissioner's Court, S. J. Callaway submitted his resignation as the county superintendent of schools for Tarrant County. He cited a lack of clerical help that made it impossible to do the job. He denied having another offer but stated that he had twice turned down more lucrative job offers. Callaway was replaced that afternoon by Leo Hammond. A newspaper article suggested that Hammond's first order of business would be to recommend S. J. Callaway for the position of chief probation officer, although Hammond refused to comment on whom he would recommend. Professor John Kooken, the superintendent of the Arlington ISD, would likely recommend F. R. Wallace of Arlington, and J. W. Cantrell, superintendent of Fort Worth ISD, would recommend J. G. Reeves of Fort Worth.[73]

On July 3, 1913, in what seems a prime example of the "good ole boy" network, S. J. Callaway was named the chief probation officer. His assistant would be S. D. Hartman.

S. J. Callaway had taught in the rural schools of Johnson County for several years. For four years starting in 1907, he was superintendent of the Polytechnic Schools. In that capacity, he took charge of a system with seven grades and seven teachers. When he resigned, he was overseer of a recognized high school and fifteen teachers. On the strength of his work in that post, he was elected county superintendent in the summer of 1912, after watching over the first Polytechnic graduating class.[74]

S. D. Hartman, his assistant, was city marshal at Tehuacana, Limestone County, for three years before coming to Fort Worth, where he served on the police force for four years. He had always been active in relief work and was familiar with the handling of juvenile delinquents.[75]

As the new probation officer, S. J. Callaway told the *Fort Worth Star-Telegram* that his philosophy was to "be a companion to the 'bad' boy. . . .Let him know you are his friend," he said, "and that you are going to help him instead of punish him. This will make a good man of him."[76]

Callaway also indicated he would install an up-to-date system of records for every child that came under his supervision. The system would be modeled after those of major metropolitan cities. He further said, "I want to erase every semblance of a court and a reformatory from juvenile correction work. I intend to work for a detention home, but this plan is vague as yet. The very word *reformatory* throws fright into a child and usually does him more harm than good. Under the new law children must not be confined with adult prisoners, but it is a bad policy to confine them in a jail even in a separate department."[77]

The new law authorized a county to create a detention home or parental school but required those counties that did not have such a home to create a separate section of the jail to serve the purpose of detention before conviction. This changed the earlier law requiring only a separate compartment. The law also allowed parents of a boy under seventeen to petition the court to commit him to the state school. The judge would then make the decision based on an evidentiary hearing. If the child was committed, parents had to agree to pay for the expense of transportation and make quarterly payments to sustain the cost of commitment. Refusal of payment terminated the commitment. The law also directed the court, on any commitment to a state school, to keep the interest of the children and their restoration to society in mind.[78]

According to the *Dallas Morning News*, Callaway also believed that "every case of juvenile delinquency should be treated individually. Some boys deserve twice as heavy punishment as others for the same technical offense. I believe in making a boy feel that I am his friend, and am seeking to help him out. Usually, he will take advantage of the opportunity to reform without being made to and as a matter of fact, compulsory reform is rarely successful. Little should be said about the bad in dealing with a boy and much should be said about the good that is in him."[79]

The article indicated Callaway had studied juvenile reform methods for several years and was a strong believer in the "modern methods" of handling juveniles. The new law gave him discretionary control over every boy under seventeen and every girl under eighteen. During the absence of the juvenile court system, another organization—the Newsboys Association of Fort Worth—had become a prominent force among juveniles in the city, and it was often antagonistic to Callaway's designs. The newsboys were primarily young boys, although some girls would join their ranks by 1914. These youths were either homeless or were helping their low-income families pay the bills by hawking newspapers. You could hear them every morning on the streets calling, "Hear ye, hear ye!" Albert C. Williams, the assistant secretary of the Cattle Raisers Association of Texas, was the president of the Newsboys Association. He regularly went to the *Fort Worth Star-Telegram* to challenge Callaway's methods and visited other juvenile probation departments in large cities such as Washington, DC; Chicago; and New York. He was particularly opposed to Callaway's plans to take photographs, which would lead to a lack of confidentiality, and to the way Callaway utilized an early, informal version of a big-brother program. Callaway wasn't passive and gave a quick retort—citing Williams's "ignorance"—when Williams questioned him publicly.[80]

Despite the new beginning for juvenile probation in 1913 and more clearly defined laws governing the treatment of juveniles, there was still no clear agreement on how best to work with juvenile offenders. The issue was gaining statewide attention. C. S. Potts, a University of Texas professor, told the Texas chapter of the National Conference of Charities and Correction that juvenile courts were "defective in the extreme." Potts, a researcher, already had some ideas about what would become an effective principle of intervention related to the risk principle—working with higher-risk youth and not having them mix with lower-risk youth, as he argued that "mixing kids with few criminal tendencies with criminals is not good."[81]

On several occasions throughout his time as chief, Callaway publicly urged the building of a separate detention home to house juveniles. He indicated that he would officially call upon the Commissioner's Court when the time was right and the court was able to support its construction. S. J. Callaway led the juvenile court for two years before accepting another post within Tarrant County as an assistant district attorney.[82]

Harvard Tarpley—the Educator

The run on educators as officers began with S. J. Callaway and continued with his successor. After a stint as the second superintendent of the Arlington Independent School System, Harvard Henry Tarpley began work as the juvenile probation officer of Tarrant County. He was the third official probation officer.[83]

H. H. Tarpley changed what Travis had started as a Sunday evening probation hour into Saturday reporting requirements for the young men on probation. As John Augustus had done, the court made a decision about which young men were likely to make the necessary changes. Many young men who came through the court went directly to Gatesville or were sent out of the big city to relatives in more rural settings. For those that got the opportunity, a contract (probation) was created for a suspended sentence to the training school, which usually included the following simple terms: report on Saturdays, stay out of trouble, and stay off the streets. A violation of this contract would typically result in commitment to the state school for an indeterminate sentence that could last no longer than the person's twenty-first birthday.[84]

H. H. Tarpley believed that "idleness is one of the chief causes contributing to delinquency," and decided to take steps to find people or businesses that might help with employment for juveniles. "Every effort is made to give the boys another chance," he said, "and they are sent to Gatesville only as a last resort." Despite his confidence in rehabilitation, Tarpley did express concern about what would happen when the juveniles were "released back home and subject to the same environment which caused them to go wrong in the first place."[85]

One of the few places where the thoughts and writings of H. H. Tarpley and his successor S. S. Ogilvie were recorded (along with an account of some of the diversity of young people they worked with) were in the case notes and letters written and kept in case files. Many of the case files were for young people on a contract, but most of those that include thoughts of the officers are for those sent on to Gatesville. Initials are used here to maintain the confidentiality of juvenile records.

Some of H. H. Tarpley's case notes: 86

*****

W. D., age 16, Virgilla Hotel, rooming house.

—this boy was kept in Mason Orphans Home at Fort Worth until he was 13 years old and became incorrigible and left the Home. He had something akin to fits—a heart trouble, and has had 24 heart attacks, and has them yet. He was sent to Abilene to be treated, but ran away. He was sent back and ran away. He takes money from his mother by force. He stole her suit case and sold it. He gave his age as 20 and later as 17. He was given 1 year sentence to the Road Gang. He had a case pending against him for stealing a watch. The mother came in and swore that the boy is now 16. Women of bad character have been kept in this rooming house possibly without knowledge of his mother, and we fear that the boy is getting in bed with them. He is addicted to drinking, reports to the saloon keeper that he is 21 years old. He is sentenced to Gatesville for not less than five years, and we will oppose his being released under that time.

*****

The following shows cooperation between neighboring counties of Tarrant and Dallas. It also reflects something other jurisdictions hardly practiced at the time—responding to the wishes of family.

F. B.—age unknown—9/4/1915

This boy lives in Dallas, come to Fort Worth, steals a messenger boys wheel. He was arrested at Arlington on his return to Dallas. He was brought before probation officers, confessed, and was placed in jail to await a hearing from his mother. His father is dead. The record we have from Dallas is that the boy has been before the probation officers there on similar charges. The mother claims that the boy has tuberculosis. We had the county health physician examine him and he presumed him in good health. In our judgement, the boy would be better off in Gatesville than loose on the world, but the pitiful plea of the mother and the fair promises of the boy caused us to release the boy to her with the following stipulations. First, the boy reported every two weeks by mail. Second, if he gets into further trouble in Fort Worth or elsewhere this probation ceases and the mother gives her word not to interfere with the disposition of the case. A copy of this report is to be furnished the Dallas Probation officers for their record.

*****

The following is a letter Tarpley sent to L. C. D.'s father, T. F. D., on 10/17/1916.

L.C.D.—Nashville, Tennessee native—runaway for 4 months.
Dear Sir,

I have your son, L C D., 14 year old, who says he has been to Chicago, St. Louis, in Ohio, Arkansas, and Southern Texas in the last four months. He had taken up with a bum of a man, and there is no telling what he has been into, or will be into if he is not taken home and cared for. He was dirty and rough looking, but shows bright and intelligent after I made him wash up. I have spent 65 cents on him, and have him locked up in the Juvenile Ward of the county jail. He has seen enough and wants to go home. Wire me a ticket, money enough for him to have something to eat on the way home, and 65 cents that the county has been out on him, and I will put him on the train and start him home. He will come home I think. He wants to go the freight train route but that is both dangerous and unlawful.

Respectfully, H. H. Tarpley.

*****

*The following comes from the case file of one of the few females referred
to the court during H. H. Tarpley's time with the court.*

N. W. May 1916.

Our attention was called to this little girl by a social worker
and friend of the family. She had been slipping off from home
and running with immoral persons. She was very incorrigible.
Her mother had to work and she had an opportunity to choose
her associates. The mother came to this office asking that we do
something to help control the girl and after looking into the case
carefully we sent her to the Home of the Good Shepherds Home.
She was transferred to the State Training School (Gainesville)
9/7/1916.

*****

G. C., age 13, 1/31/19.

G. has been in this office four different times in each case
charged with running away from home would not mind his
Parents when his Father tries to whip him he will run off and
stay until picked up by officers and turned over to his Father. He
has a verry high temper and resents verry much being punished
when in School and complains that he does not get fir treatment
which I think is imaginary on his part. He seems to have trouble
getting along with his Step Mother has the idear she does not
treat him right. He has been running with E. D. who has a verry
bad reputation for running away from home E. has also been
in this office several times charged with stealing and being
incorrigible. The last time G. was brought to this office he was
released by Judge Small and given one more chance. The home
conditions are not what they should be there is room from
improvement on both sides. Unless there is a considerable in
the near future he will be Gatesville bound. I have instructed
him when he has trouble of any kind to come to this Office for
advise and not lay out at night away from home there has been
nothing left undone to straighten this boy out. – H. H. Tarpley

*****

C. C.—Hispanic [one of few in these files]. 8/6/1915.

This boy's mother lives in Brownsville. He never knew his father. He was placed with his uncle Yeana Tijerino in Fort Worth to live. In July 1915 he ran away from him and on the far side of town on the way to Brownsville. He was given lodging and after spending a few days he was asked to return to his uncle. He refused. He feared his uncle because he had insulted a white lady by exposing his person and talking disrespectfully to her. He was brought to this office and talked to. His uncle agreed to send him to his mother with a stockman in a few weeks. The boy agreed to stay and obey him. Not to run away anymore. His mother was notified, but replied as his uncle said, that she could not control him. She said keep him. He ran away again. He stopped at a workmen's camp twenty miles from Fort Worth. We were notified, sent after him, but in the darkness he got away from the officer. His uncle went out after him and brought him to this office. On 8/11/15, he was given an indefinite sentence to Gatesville. His uncle is an excellent Mexican, but like all Mexicans is too severe in his punishment.

H. H. Tarpley worked in the juvenile court for approximately four years, until retiring on November 26, 1918. He was assisted in the work initially by Miss Florence Dibrell of Polytechnic, who worked without pay; later by Mrs. Ollie Hargraves, a former police matron; and finally by Harry Hamilton, who resigned alongside his chief.

Tarpley got his real estate license after leaving, but eventually went back into education. He taught for some time at North Side High School in Fort Worth before departing to East Texas. In Tarpley's obituary, a friend described him in this way: "It is because of such personalities as was his that civilization continues to advance. He lived right, according to his highest sense. He was always working for the good of the schools, the church, and the community in general." H. H. Tarpley was the third in what would be a long line of quality leadership for the court.

S. S. (Sam) Ogilvie

Just three days after H. H. Tarpley's retirement in 1918, S. S. Ogilvie was appointed to the position. S. S. largely continued the work of Tarpley and maintained Saturday reporting for the juveniles in the system. A compulsory attendance officer was assigned to work with Ogilvie during his time with the department.[87] Possibly because the event was held in Fort Worth and the Tarrant County judge was president of the association, Ogilvie gained a statewide presence when he provided a speech to the County Judges and Commissioners Association of Texas in 1921. The topic was the "Terror of Juvenile Delinquents."[88] Ogilvie was also called as a witness by a specially appointed legislative committee investigating conditions at the state training schools.[89] There is very little additional information about his tenure. The record of his work is largely found in historical notes and letters.[90]

Some of S. S. Ogilvie's case notes:

*****

On 12/28/21 S. S. Ogilvie wrote a letter to the US Navy recruiting office, trying to help the young man get a fresh start.

F. A.—age 14—Kansas City—both parents dead—notes written on 5/24/1919

—This boy claims to have no family anywhere.

Gentlemen:

This is to inform you that F. A. has been under the jurisdiction of juvenile court of this county since the 24th day of May, 1919. Upon investigation of his case, we found that he had no living mother or father, any brothers or sisters or any other relatives that we know of. While there was no charge other than being an incorrigible boy drifting around over the country from place to place. We felt that it would be to his advantage to have him committed to the Juvenile Training School, where he would receive some much needed education. For the above stated reasons he was sent to our state training school. He has now been released, and wishes to enlist in the Navy, to which I have no objection. The records of my office according to his statement will show that he will be eighteen years of age on the 5th day of September 1932. Mr. C. E. King, Supt. of Boys Training School informs me that he made a splendid record while in his institution.

I am, very respectfully, SS Ogilvie

*****

N. A. - 6/15/17, age 10. Take from the possession of Mrs. Simmons 3 dollars without consent. Stole 50 cents from another. Was out all night and was going with the circus.

*****

A letter from SS Ogilvie to State Training School Superintendent—a recommendation for parole for a young man when a possible suitable family has been located.

June 10, 1920
Dr. Mr. King (CE),
In case of N. A. Col. Who has been in your care for about three years, will advise that arrangements have been made with a colored man and his wife by the name of Walker who live in this city, and have no children to take this boy and give him a good home and see that the boy is properly looked after. If in your opinion he is ready for parole, I will recommend same which you can forward to me and I will have filled out and returned to you.
Very respectfully. SS Ogilvie.

*****

The following letter was written to C. E. King of the training school on August 12, 1921, on behalf of a young man whose parents want him home. At the age of twelve, on April 15, 1918, H. G. had stolen a five-dollar watch. Interestingly, the child's involvement in a pro-social activity, the marching band, seems to be a barrier to his release.

Dear Mr. King,
Sometime back I wrote you in regard to parole of H. G. In reply to this letter you stated he was a member of the boys band, and in so much they had many dates to fill during the months of June and July. You thought it would be worth much to remain there during this time this information I have given to Mr. and Mrs. Gray. Mr. Gray was in to see me this morning and if it should meet with your approval they are verry anxious to have H.G. come home in time to have a few days at home before placing him in school this fall. Will be glad to know what you

think of paroling him at this time.

I am very respectful, SS Ogilvie.

Response from CE King—August 16, 1920—
Dear Mr. Ogilvie—
Answering your favor with regard to the release of H. G., will say that band has several more trips to make though I shall try to send H.G. home in time to begin school this fall term. I would be glad to have you let me know just when your school term in Fort Worth commences next month.

Yours very truly, CE King.

*****

In this letter on a case opened on April 12, 1919, the probation officer seems to be corresponding in an effort to keep the young man from facing further trouble during his parole from the state system. The following is a letter from S. S. Ogilvie to J. F.'s father dated February 9, 1922.

Dear Sir,

I have just received letter from Miss Bertha Trotter, Parole officer at Training School informing me that you have failed to send in your monthly report since November 1st. which as you should understand is a violation of instruction given you when sent home and it is imperative that you should attend to this matter in order to not have Mr. King or the new Superintendent recall you. Must insist that you fill out your December and January reports that present them to me to be approved without further delay.

I am very respectfully, SS Ogilvie

*****

L. D. – 15 – April 1919 case file –
The following letter is from C. E. King, the superintendent at Gatesville State Training School, to S. S. Ogilvie on July 24, 1920. It concerns L. D., age fifteen when his case was opened in April of 1919. King seems to indicate that the state system is becoming aggravated by requests for release from probation officials.

Dear Mr. Ogilvie,

I have your favor of the 21st institution just received, and in answer wish to thank you for your expression of a desire for cooperation in the matter of handling juveniles. I feel sure that you wish to handle the matter just as we try to do, for the best interest of all boys and that means of course that all must be treated alike. The old subterfuge of moving out of the state or moving out to a farm has been worked to death from points all over the state for the past few months. Almost without an exception where a release has been secured on this ground, we find that the move is a very temporary affair and the boy is back in his old surroundings with no strings on him. Then the correspondence picks up with parents who have boys still in the institution and see the other boy roaming the streets. I feel sure that by cooperation in the matter we can save you considerable annoyance as well as the institution and at the same time give such boys the training they need and require them to carry fair with the other boys.

With best wishes,

I am, yours very truly, CE King.

SS writes back on August 2 to say the family is in fact moving to Los Angeles and that he is requesting parole.

*****

The following letter is to John P. Plover, probation officer from Santarosa, California, in response to a Western Union telegram regarding L. F., whose case file was opened on December 19, 1917. The letter is dated January 21, 1922. In it, the probation officer is asking that California intervene where Texas has been unable to gain much ground.

Dear Sir,

Your two wires of recent date in regard to L. F. have been received. I have taken the matter up with Father of the boy, Mr. J.W. F* * * in regard to having the boy returned home. Mr. F * * * is just a common ordinary laborer and states to us that he is not in a position to send the money for his ticket. Will further state that this boy has been handled quite a number of times by Probation officers of this county, dating back as far as December

1917. I think that he is one of the worst bicycle thieves I have ever had anything to do with. He was committed to the Training school early in the year of 1919 and was sent there. He was examined by the physician of this institution and found to have trecoma of the eye, which according to statement made to me is uncurable and contagious, for this reason he was released to us. Therefore, if he should fall into our hands again we would be at a loss as to what to do with him. If there is anything or anyway that you could confine him this county would be pleased for you to do so, for we cannot handle him here. Give this matter your immediate attention and let us hear what you think in the matter.

I am yours very truly, SS Ogilvie.

*****

In the following letter to the state school, Ogilvie writes in regard to W. C., whose case was opened on February 14, 1919. The juvenile was "stealing automobiles and joyriding, stealing, forged checks for $120." Ogilvie is trying to keep the father from filing for relief from the court.

Some time back Mr. C***, the father of W. C., whom you have in your charge, came to my office and discussed the proposition of going into the courts with Habeas Corpus proceedings, for the purpose of getting his boy from your institution. At that time I used my influence to have him not do this, for as you well know we scarcely ever win out in these cases, regardless of all regularity in our cases. In order to get around this proposition, I promised Mr. C. I would take this matter up with you, and see what could be done in getting W.C. paroled in time to enter school this fall. Therefore, I am writing this letter for this purpose.

The following letter from C. E. King to Ogilvie indicates that the boy will be recommitted out of Coryell County.

If his people give you any more worry about this matter, you may advise them that we are holding the boy on a commitment from Coryell County.

The following was then forwarded to Mr. C from S. S. Ogilvie:

Attached you will find a letter from Mr. King, dated 8/20/20, which I have just received, and will fully explain to you Mr. King's action and ideas. Therefore W.C.'s case is entirely out of the hands of Tarrant County Officials, and will have to be taken up with Mr. EB McMordie, PO of Coryell, Texas. There is nothing I am able to do at this time.

S. S. Ogilvie held the position for four years, leaving in 1922, but he remained a familiar figure in the courthouse, taking the position of deputy chief of the District Clerk's office of Tarrant County. He remained in this position until shortly before his passing.

Ogilvie's death at the age of sixty-one was as tragic as it was mysterious. In October of 1932 he was found lying face down in the Clear Fork of the Trinity River, his throat slashed; the unlikely ruling was suicide. It was a sad end to a life dedicated to service. In poor health, he had retired from the district clerk's office just two months before.[91]

C. E. Baker: The Quiet Period

C. E. Baker took over the reins as chief probation officer in 1923. He remained in the position through 1937. Very few details are available regarding Baker's tenure, with a few surviving records showing only salary information. Baker continued the tradition of being active in state organizations; he was a founding member of the Texas Probation Association and was assigned to the first legislative committee.[92] There is one newspaper article that suggests he had a limited understanding of evidence-based practices and research; in it he attributes the building of playgrounds at the county schools to a decrease in juvenile crime and a rise in morale among the inmates.[93]

R. E. (Bob) Neely

R. E. Neely was the chief probation officer from 1937 to late 1946. In 1943, there were major revisions to the Juvenile Court Act, and parts of the act were repealed. It was at this time that the Juvenile Court of Texas became a mix of civil and criminal law and procedure, with an emphasis on civil procedures.[94]

It was during Neely's tenure, in March 1944, that Tarrant County Judge Clarence Kraft insisted that the Texas Behavioral Commission launch a formal investigation into abuse allegations at the Gatesville school. Judge Kraft had committed a young man who had tried to escape the state facility. The boy was trying to escape with another youth. They were caught and beaten. The other boy was beaten so badly that he required hospitalization. The TBC did investigate but were initially more concerned with how Judge Kraft knew about the events. The school sociologist who leaked information to Judge Kraft soon became the subject of a sexual abuse investigation and resigned.[95]

Neely was the chief during a time when juvenile crime began to rise rather sharply. A *Dallas Morning News* article on March 27, 1943, indicated that Tarrant County had seen a 20 percent rise in referrals during the previous year. There is little else known about Bob Neely's tenure.[96]

FOUR

The Anchors

In an era when the ideological and political makeup of the juvenile court is a river with an ever-changing current, the most recent five probation officers can be considered anchors for the juvenile work of Tarrant County. So much so that for a time it was believed they were the only five directors the department had ever known.

The Hoss: Lynn W. Ross

On December 4, 1946, a decision was made in Texas to bring in a new kind of probation officer. Despite the progressive nature of juvenile court work in Texas and the reformers who brought the ideal into existence, the work had been seen, and in many jurisdictions today is still seen, as a quasi-criminal-justice arena and has therefore long attracted those interested in law enforcement careers. Even today, ideas that are central to juvenile justice reform—that juveniles should be handled in the community, and that punishment not only has no impact, but in many cases is detrimental to the rehabilitation of youth—are viewed with skepticism. In Texas, in criminal justice, and even in juvenile justice, the tenets of social work are viewed as somewhat soft on the issue of crime. What would social work have to do with someone named Hoss?[97]

In December 1946, at the age of thirty-six, Lynn W. Ross, also known affectionately as Hoss Ross, was hired by Tarrant County to begin work in January 1947. He would usher in an era of stability for Tarrant County Juvenile Services. Ross would serve in the post for three decades and establish a new kind of model.

Lynn Ross was different from many in the juvenile court system in that he wanted to work with disadvantaged children from the very beginning of his career. He didn't find the work later in life or have a change of plans. As his son would later say, he devoted his life to helping kids.

Ross was a child of the Great Depression in South Texas. Though he had to wait until his twenties to begin college, he was the first child in his family to graduate. Through his athleticism and hard work, Ross put himself through college at Texas State University in Georgetown, Texas, in the 1930s. He was a football player, but his scholarship only existed while football was in season. He was occasionally able to get a scholarship by playing an off-season sport but would often have to quit school during the off-season to work, only to return again on a football scholarship.[98]

The young man graduated college in six years, and he and his wife moved to Corsicana to serve as directors of the boys at the state orphanage. In the 1940s, Ross decided he wanted to continue his education but did not take the traditional route of a man who wanted to work in juvenile justice. Even so, his choice of schools put him in a place that would plant the dream. Ross chose to get his master's in social work in Chicago, Illinois, the birthplace of the juvenile court in the United States.[99]

Ross was drafted into the US Navy while he was still finishing his studies. He started the two-year master's program in 1940, and before he finished, World War II had begun. On December 7, 1941, Pearl Harbor drew the United States into the struggle. Ross began serving his country upon his graduation in 1942.[100]

Upon his release from service, Ross took a position in Dallas County's juvenile court as the assistant chief probation officer. Within a year a position opened up "where the West begins." Ross applied and was chosen over thirty-five other applicants as the director for Tarrant County Juvenile Services. Tarrant County would have a leader for years to come.[101]

Ross was a social worker at heart and believed in the value of education. Upon starting in 1947, he saw the detriment to young people when they were placed in the juvenile ward of the county jail. The sheriff's office ran the jail, and although matrons occasionally looked after the young delinquents in their care, the environment was not a healthy one. Ross spent the next three decades championing the building of a separate juvenile detention center for kids.[102]

Lynn Ross believed in an educated workforce. With some exceptions—officers who brought a specific skill or who had an outstanding ability to connect with youth—he required his officers to have at least a bachelor's degree, with a few exceptions. He had this requirement almost four decades before the state system followed suit—another model from this Texas county.[103]

Essentially, all of the landmark juvenile case rulings occurred during Lynn Ross's tenure. He had a unique perspective on many of the cases in that his son, Lynn Ross Jr., was in law school during that time. Lynn Jr. remembers talking to his father specifically about the *Gault* decision in 1967. They were reading the findings together when his father said, "This is going to tie our hands in doing what is best for children." At first glance, this seems an odd statement regarding something that would afford more rights to kids, but in essence Ross agreed with the dissenter, Justice Stewart: this would move the juvenile court system more into alignment with adult court and take away its informality. His comment also revealed Ross's level of commitment: his first reaction was to consider *what is best for children*.[104]

Mr. Ross: that is what those who knew him still call him. Not Lynn, not Ross: Mister Ross. His name, long after his passing, still commands respect. (Mr. Ross passed away in 1989 at the age of 79.) While the agency was relatively small, Mr. Ross was sitting in on every interview of new staff. He commanded instant respect by his mere presence, but also through his not-so-subtle messages. Ross not only expected an educated staff, but a staff that respected authority. He was a conservative man, and maybe in a sign of the times, he expected someone to look the part of an authority figure. When Charlie Jones (eventually a thirty-year veteran of the department) appeared at the department for his interview, he had fairly long hair. While he was waiting outside of Ross's office for an interview, Ross entered the area and said to the secretary, "If I was here for an interview, I'd probably make sure I had a good haircut." Ross reentered his office, and Jones quickly departed for the nearest barber. Upon returning, Jones got the interview and the job. Some years later, Vince Herdman appeared for an interview and had been given some warning about his hair. He still had his mustache. One of the questions Ross asked was about the facial hair: "How attached are you to the mustache?"

Herdman responded, "I've had it since I got out of the military, but if it is the difference in getting this job or not, I'll shave it today, sir." Herdman got the job and got to keep the mustache. It was the principle of the matter for Ross. He wanted officers who looked professional, and he wanted officers that respected authority.[105]

Ross had another unusual impact on Tarrant County Juvenile Services: three generations of his family contributed to the work and the dream of the department. His son, Lynn Jr., met his wife at the department while his father was the director (she was a probation officer), and Ross's grandson worked in the detention center while studying to be a lawyer.[106]

Ross was popular among his peers for a lot of reasons, and he worked very hard. He suffered a heart attack in 1957. At that time there was no air conditioning in the civil courts building, but when he returned from medical leave a window unit was installed in his office. He became even more popular, as all the judges in the building began to frequent his office, especially on summer afternoons.[107]

"If you see a frog on a fencepost, someone helped it get there" is a phrase that Jerry Wood, hired by Ross and later made assistant director, attributed to Ross. He was a father figure, a very paternal man who wanted the best for his employees and the kids they worked to help. This is also evident in another of his nicknames: "Big Daddy." He wasn't very hands-on with the direct care of the kids, but he was involved in all decisions connected to getting workers and young people what they needed. Among many examples, Herdman, a thirty-four-year veteran of the department, recalled a time that Ross drove him and another young employee to the city of Austin so they could get their child- and youth-worker licenses for overseeing facilities for juveniles. It's as if he didn't want those in his care getting lost in the big city.[108]

Ross even mentored those who came afterwards. Carey Cockerell remembers getting to know and share stories with Ross after Cockerell became the director in 1984. One of those stories involved some of the residents of the State Orphans' Home in Corsicana, where Ross had been the director in the 1930s. The orphanage neighbored a nearby farmer who had a watermelon patch. Some of the kids decided they would raid this patch, take a watermelon, and later celebrate by eating their spoils. Not getting caught the first time made it even more enticing. As it was rare to get one over on Ross, they repeated this several times. At a reunion with Ross later in life, they chuckled in the retelling of how they had finally pulled the wool over his eyes. Ross smiled broadly and got the last laugh, as he told them the real story: The farmer had complained to Ross after the first melon was taken. Lynn Ross took responsibility and paid the farmer for the melon and the entire patch. "So you see," he told the former orphans, "you were stealing from yourselves all that time."[109]

Ross was not a major advocate of training because he believed in hiring an educated professional who was equipped to hit the ground running. His requirement for degreed professionals in probation was ahead of his time, but his requirement for those working in detention to have degrees as well continues to remain unique in Texas.[110]

Ross, after accomplishing his career-long desire of creating a detention center for juveniles, retired from work at Tarrant County Juvenile Services in 1977 but did not retire from helping young people. He left the Tarrant County post to take on the challenge of working at the All Church Home for Children (currently ACH Child and Family Services) in Fort Worth. This was a residential home for young people in need of a second chance. Even in retirement, he worked for the dream.[111]

Ross came to the department with a master's degree in social work and brought that emphasis to Tarrant County. He believed in helping young people in the settings in which they lived from day to day, and required his officers to visit with probationers in those environments. The visits took place in the homes and at the schools where youth were enrolled. While many departments require the offenders and their families to make office visits, these home and school visits by probation officers are an uncommon feature that is still in place in Tarrant County today.[112]

The Professor: Paul Cromwell 1977-1984

It is hard, if not almost impossible, to follow an icon. Lynn Ross had the longest tenure by far of any chief in Tarrant County. He had a paternal leadership style and brought sweeping and significant changes to the juvenile court. In short, who in their right mind would be next?

Paul Cromwell had been the board director for the Texas Board of Pardons and Paroles prior to taking the helm at juvenile services at the age of thirty-four. He was looking for something different. He had only been on the pardons and paroles board for two years, with less than a year as chair. He had spent the two previous years as a federal probation officer. While he had some experience as an adjunct professor, and four years of professional and practical experience in criminal justice, he did not have a specific background in working with juveniles.[113]

Nonetheless, it was during his tenure in 1979 that the National Association of Counties (NACo) presented Tarrant County Juvenile Services with the Juvenile Achievement Award for its outstanding work with juveniles. At the time, NACo was composed of just fewer than three thousand counties nationwide. This award was featured in the *Dallas Morning News*, and Jerry Wood indicated that NACo was "most impressed" with the overall flow of cases, from detention screening to the way young people were supervised in the community.[114]

In 1981 the department got some additional national exposure. A CBS film crew shot a *Schoolbreak Special* in the Dallas area. Chris Sarandon, well known in his own right but perhaps better known as the brother of Susan Sarandon, starred in the film about a juvenile services director trying to find homes for abandoned foster kids. The episode, "Broken Promises," was filmed in several locations, including Tarrant County's juvenile detention center.[115]

Cromwell held a master's degree and taught classes at Texas Christian University during his time with juvenile services. Upon leaving Tarrant County, he pursued his doctorate and has been in academia, teaching and publishing in criminal justice ever since. It was also during his tenure that the Texas Juvenile Probation Commission began in 1981, in part to establish requirements that include formal training and certification of probation officers throughout the state. An educator at heart, Cromwell brought this emphasis to the department where it had been lacking.[116]

Cromwell focused on high-quality training for the staff at Tarrant County Juvenile Services, and a training manual was written for the department during his tenure. Here is an excerpt of case management philosophy taken from this manual, which has continued to guide the department:

> In general methods are directed toward helping the probationer mobilize his strengths and assets in the pursuit of his own goals in ways not in conflict with society. The emphasis is on casework, and not merely surveillance. . . . The emphasis is not on telling the probationer what he should do, but on helping him to make realistic plans for himself—realistic in the sense of being possible within his capacities and alternatives—and encouraging him in his attempts to carry them out. Each probationer is a unique person, and there is not one probation program that is most suitable for all probationers. Plans for each probationer must be individualized to some degree and visualized within the particular subculture in which the probationer lives. . . . How much the probationer changes in the direction

desired by the probation officer depends on how much the probationer wants to change. . . . The probation officer cannot force lasting and effective change in a probationer, but he can be influential.[117]

Cromwell's tenure with the department was also distinguished by some reorganization. When he began, there were 127 staff members in the department, but these included child welfare staff (child welfare, child support, and so on). Such services were finally separated from probation work, and a staff of eighty-two probation workers moved in 1977 from offices in downtown Fort Worth to offices adjoining the detention center in its current location.[118]

At the time of his hiring, an intake staff was in place to handle court cases, receive new cases, and send clients ordered to probation out to field officers. Cromwell combined these staffs into four distinct teams with one supervisor, two intake officers, and four field officers per team. This provided some continuity between intake and field staff.[119]

Cromwell left the department under difficult circumstances after technically getting a vote of no confidence from his staff on April 4, 1984. There was also a Juvenile Board investigation. He was not asked to leave, but decided it would be better for the staff and the young people of the county if new leadership were in place.[120]

The Interim: Jerry Wood 1984

Jerry Wood did not serve long and was not permanently assigned, but he did spend four months as the interim director of the department. Mr. Wood's career with the juvenile department spans almost four decades, in addition to his time as an intern with the department in the 1960s when he was a student at Texas Christian University. He served as the interim director from April 4, 1984, to September 1, 1984. Hired by Lynn Ross, he spent much of his early career as supervisor over intake; then, early in Paul Cromwell's tenure, he was promoted to assistant director, a post he held for nearly thirty years. After serving as interim director, he returned to his post as assistant director and held it for all but one of Carey Cockerell's years of service. If not for some health issues, he would likely still be serving the juveniles of Tarrant County. He had that sort of passion for the job—no, make that the dream.[121]

Wood is what you might call a character. He has a sharp wit and is always ready with a story. He is also a sports fanatic and has a collection of sports memorabilia in his home that overflows from a designated sports room filled long ago. Wood had an uncanny knack for being able to connect with kids by memorizing every area high school sports mascot. Walking the halls of Tarrant County Juvenile Services with him, you likely heard some version of the following, "Where do you go to school young man?" with the youth responding, "I go to L.D. Bell High School, sir." Mr. Wood would connect with, "So you're a Blue Raider. Did you know where your school got that mascot?"

Jerry's father, Lawrence Wood, was a longtime officer with the Fort Worth Police Department (FWPD). Lawrence Wood was eventually the captain of the traffic division and was very attached to his Harley-Davidson motorcycle, which he rode until his retirement. (The motorcycle still sits in the training department for the FWPD.) Lawrence often had traffic duty on University Drive, and the kids who were cruising called him Woody. They remember him gaining respect by giving it.

Jerry remembers he occasionally accompanied his father to his workplace and learned invaluable lessons about what it means to serve in a position of public safety. One such lesson was about the difference between control and authority. He was at the jail one day as a very young man when he saw an officer having to get physical with an inmate. The officer was able to get the better of the inmate and control the situation. Jerry remarked to another officer in the area, "Now, that is a police officer." What happened next remains embedded in Wood's memory even today: the officer grabbed him by the collar and walked him into another area where an officer was quietly directing a compliant inmate. "Now you see, son, *that* is a police officer!"[122]

Wood also remembers going to a luncheon event with Lynn Ross at Ridglea Presbyterian Church. The lunch was really good, and it was free. Ross was the scheduled speaker, but when he took the microphone he announced that they would not be hearing from him, but from "one of the sharpest young minds in juvenile justice." Wood perked up, wondering what sort of wisdom this person would share with the group, only to be startled further by the words, "And now here is Mr. Jerry Wood." Wood gave a speech, and after glad-handing the patrons with Ross, they walked toward the exit. Wood didn't say anything, but gave Ross a look to which Ross responded, "Jerry, always remember, there is no such thing as a free lunch."[123]

It is not as if Jerry needed to hear these words. He gave everything to his work. He usually arrived before anyone else, and left long after the end of the workday. Despite being a director with an interim moniker, he remains an icon of the department. He also taught in an adjunct capacity at two local universities: Texas Christian University and Texas Wesleyan University. Outside his influence at the department, many criminal justice majors throughout the decades were taught juvenile justice by Jerry Wood. A TCU graduate himself, Wood helped many frogs "up on that fence."[124]

The Professional: Carey Cockerell

If it is hard to follow an icon, it may be even harder to bring calm to an organization after some upheaval. Carey Cockerell was a native of Tarrant County. He originally left to pursue an education in youth ministry. He received his Undergraduate degree from Ouachita Baptist University in Arkansas and went on to Louisville, Kentucky, to receive his degree from Southern Seminary. Prior to leaving Texas, Cockerell had never even heard of juvenile justice. He had a roommate who was working for the state reception center for juvenile delinquents in Kentucky, however, and the roommate informed him that there was a job opening as the recreation director. Cockerell got the job and received his master's in social work from the University of Louisville while working at the state school.

The Vietnam War was in full swing, and as he neared the completion of his graduate degree, Cockerell decided to take matters into his own hands and enlist, only to have the draft end a few months later. He was sent to Fort Bragg to train. Because of his background, he was quickly put in a position counseling trainees. He served two years in the military, fulfilling his service requirement.[125]

At that point Cockerell came back to his home state. He was offered a position as the assistant superintendent of the Brownwood State School in the Texas Youth Council system. This was in 1974, during the height of the *Morales v. Turman* case which shook the foundations of TYC. Carey Cockerell, at the age of twenty-seven, was a part of the "new blood" brought in to the broken system. He learned on the job about bringing calm to a system in turmoil and worked in the state school system for ten years.[126]

In 1984, Cockerell decided to make a change, partly because of his frustrations with a system that wanted to treat every kid and every facility the same way, and partly because of an opportunity that arose closer to home, in Tarrant County. On September 1, 1984, Cockerell became the director of Tarrant County Juvenile Services. Much like he was asked to do in TYC, he ushered in needed changes and helped bring calm to a brewing storm.[127]

Carey Cockerell had to deal with an agency divided over the loss of its last leader and the resulting tensions between staff over which side each had taken during that time. Those loyal to Cromwell were on the losing side and resentful he was gone. Those wanting him gone resented the remnants of his leadership. Cockerell remembered a staff meeting with his supervisors some two to four years in, when he could still feel this tension: "I had to stop the meeting and lay it on the table."

Cockerell told his staff they had a tough choice to make. They could agree to move forward or decide that they couldn't. He didn't continue with a speech about what their decisions would mean, or ask them to mull it over. In the moment, he went down the line and asked each person to make his or her decision known. Every manager articulated to him, and the group, a readiness to move forward. "I felt like that was a turning point for the organization," Cockerell recalled.[128]

With the commitment of leadership in hand, Cockerell set out to bring about changes. He had taken over soon after the creation of the Texas Juvenile Probation Commission, the state agency overseeing probation in Texas. Now there was a counterpart to the state agency overseeing institutions, so the playing field had leveled. This ushered in a new funding stream for community-based juvenile justice, and Carey proved to be very innovative at leveraging those dollars for effective systems to help keep young people in their communities. During Cockerell's tenure, many of those dollars were earmarked to provide counties with additional officers, and the staff in Tarrant County grew rather quickly. Cockerell expanded on the team concept initiated by Paul Cromwell. He separated out the intake unit again and placed geographically based field teams in the community rather than in the main offices. He wanted them to get to know the community and the resources available to the kids who lived in particular areas.[129]

Cockerell went to Weatherford, along with other juvenile justice officials in the area, to State Representative Ric Williamson's home. Williamson would be in a position to ask the state for money in community corrections. Representative Williamson asked those in the room what the number would need to be to make a difference. They gave him a number. It was precisely the amount eventually appropriated by the legislature, and with very few strings attached. The community-probation side of juvenile justice would now be able to find services.[130]

Early on, in July 1988, Cockerell brought Mike Slimp over from the County Information Technology department to be a member of Juvenile Services. He immediately started working on a computerized case management system, and by June 1989, the KIDS case management system was implemented. The system, along with computer terminals, brought the department forward with the use of technology, and the platform served as the case management system for over two decades.[131]

In the early 1990s, Cockerell's innovations further established Tarrant County Juvenile Services as a model for others across the state, the country, and even across the pond. In 1992, Cockerell began looking for a program that would help his officers make a difference with those young people who were on the verge of mandatory separation from the community. He found such a program in the Youth Advocacy Program (YAP) in Pennsylvania. This program was an in-home intervention that paired mentors with troubled kids, a sort of intensive big brother-big sister program with salaried mentors. Cockerell convinced the founders of the program, when they implemented these services in Tarrant County, to recruit mentors within the zip codes where the young people lived and to require a no-refusal policy among the providers so that every child referred to the program would be helped, regardless of background or offense. These requirements ensured mentors who were invested in the community, and offered young people models who had experienced some of the life that they had lived. YAP describes the program in the following way on their website:

> YAP's mission is to engage human service systems so that they rely less on institutional care and to invest more in supporting families and neighborhoods. They currently work with child welfare, juvenile justice, behavioral health, disability, and education systems to develop and offer community-based alternatives for the highest risk children, young people, young adults, and families. The staff seeks to capitalize on the strength and resources of families and communities, including identifying and engaging the natural helpers that are found in every community to support the highest risk youth and families.[132]

Cockerell furthered efforts to partner intensively with local service organizations similarly invested in helping to solve the problems of young people and their families. From the beginning, the model of the juvenile justice program had included the doctrine of *parens patraie*—the idea that the state had the authority to intervene when parents were providing inadequate care and supervision. This led to a growth in institutions where the state took over this function entirely. In many cases in early juvenile justice, the parent was seen as the problem, not as part of the solution. Institutions were placed in rural locations far from the communities of most families, in part strategically, to separate young people from the problems of their community and families.[133]

The short-sighted part of this doctrine is that unless kept to adulthood, which happened in many cases, the child would always return to the parents. The practice of removing the child from the family might be helpful when stabilization was needed in the short term, but a better model might be to provide families with the tools to deal with their own problems and provide better care and supervision of their children. Cockerell initiated a contract with the Lena Pope Home in Fort Worth to offer family preservation services. This involved a family interventionist working in the home with the entire family to bring about basic changes within the family.[134]

The history of the Lena Pope Home started with a family. This is the history of that family as listed on the website:

> Since 1930, Mrs. Pope set high expectations of the children who sought assistance from the Home. Countless young lives learned a value system and a sense of personal responsibility, thanks to those standards established so long ago. That same value system and those standards have continued to influence the young lives entrusted to us because of the commitment of the Board of Directors and staff of the Home.... While the definition of our programs has changed and the mission of Lena Pope Home, Inc. has taken on many new and diversified tasks, the role of developing young people to their full potential as conscientious citizens has endured through the decades.[135]

Both the family preservation program and YAP were offered in the homes—with the families as partners—and included a close working relationship with the probation officer. This was a more complete system of care and became a model for the country. It also became a model for other countries. The juvenile justice system in the United States borrowed heavily from English common law, so in a sort of reversal, England and other countries began to pay attention to what was working in the United States, including in Tarrant County.

Carey Cockerell gives much of the credit for what worked in Tarrant County Juvenile Services during his tenure to the leadership of Judge Scott Moore. He and Moore worked in partnership, and Cockerell remembers the judge coming into his office every morning carrying a detention log that detailed the status of each young person in detention. Judge Moore had notes and ideas about how to move forward expeditiously in each case. He was truly concerned for the welfare of young people.[136]

Reform employs many methods, but education is an essential element for young people whether or not they are involved in the juvenile justice system. There was a time up until the early nineties when delinquent young people were at risk for being removed from the school system—a social system in itself—and that meant a total removal. If you got expelled from schools in Texas in the early 1990s, you were expelled to the streets. This changed in Tarrant County when Judge Moore and Carey Cockerell were called to a meeting about the issue in 1993.

A young man had been suspended from school and was sitting at home. A complaint from the community that this was detrimental to his success got Judge Moore's attention, and not much more was necessary. He organized a group of professionals to attack the problem, and within about two months, an educational system tailored to these youth was created. Moore's innovation spurred the creation of a legislatively mandated Juvenile Justice Alternative Education Program in Texas in 1995 so that young people accused of delinquent conduct could still get an education.[137]

Having worked inside the state school system in Texas, Cockerell often found himself frustrated by his inability to predict which kids in his care would not make it after their release. He had kids do extremely well in the system, and kids who really struggled, and often those with the most potential were unable to make it and returned to the system. To make lasting change, he felt it took responsible adults in the community working together to help young people realize their potential and to keep them from further penetrating the justice system. In 1995, additional funding was made available to local juvenile probation departments, but in a move that ran counter to his colleagues' inclinations, one that would surprise many inside and outside the system and would continue to set Tarrant County apart, Cockerell turned down millions of dollars from the state. Why?

In 1995, political attitudes ran toward a "get tough" approach based on beliefs about the rise of juvenile crime, in particular a belief in the rise of a whole class of "morally deficient" juveniles. Reflecting those beliefs, the 74th Texas Legislature authorized a budget that would assist juvenile authorities, but with strings attached: the funds were to be used to build institutions based on a "boot camp" model at the local level.[138]

Tarrant County's appropriation of that funding would have been between three and four million dollars. Who says no to that kind of money? No one in the state of Texas did, with one exception. Tarrant County, under the leadership of Carey Cockerell, turned heads by turning it down. Cockerell and the rest of the leadership looked at the research about the boot camp model and post-adjudication facilities that the appropriation specified, and learned that not only did this type of program have little impact but that running such facilities would cost the department tens of millions of dollars in the long term. Thanks, but no thanks. This proved to be a wise financial move for the department. It also kept Tarrant County's system operating according to its philosophy of rehabilitation and further embedded the practice of using available resources to enhance community-based care.[139]

In April 1998, a Public Broadcasting Service (PBS) documentary featured Tarrant County's juvenile justice system as an example of innovative approaches that work without a need to remove youth from the community. "Tarrant County . . . has designed its programs with the goal of identifying problems and providing . . . interventions at the earliest point," series producer and criminologist Roger Graef said. The county reduces juvenile violence by providing "the most extensive set of options for judges I've yet seen," he said.[140]

Cockerell's direction brought additional attention throughout the state and nationally. In a study released in 2000 by Richard Mendel, a researcher for the nonpartisan American Youth Policy Forum in Washington, DC, Tarrant County was recognized for having built "perhaps the most impressive array of community-based alternatives to detention and out-of-home placements in the nation." The publication was titled *Less Hype, More Help*, and it was about what works and what doesn't in reducing juvenile crime. The report detailed the struggle of juvenile justice, and indicated that most counties and states, despite having the information and resources to make a positive impact, deal with juvenile crime by passing legislation for services that either aren't known to work or actually may increase recidivism.[141]

In 2001 Richard Mendel followed up on the previous study by publishing another document, *Less Cost, More Safety—Guiding Lights for Reform in Juvenile Justice,* through the American Youth Policy Forum. Tarrant County's juvenile probation agency is profiled as one of eight "lighthouse programs in the country worthy of emulating. Its emphasis on treatment and community-based supervision is far more successful than the 'lock 'em up and throw away the key' approach used in most other Texas counties," Mendel wrote.[142] This follow-up report continues to raise awareness about promising approaches and may help show other jurisdictions how to reform juvenile justice.

In 2003, the Coalition for Juvenile Justice, a national nonprofit advisory-advocacy group on juvenile justice issues, highlighted juvenile detention reform in a section titled "Unlocking the Future" in its annual advisory report. The report looked at the implications of what appeared to be a national overreliance on detention or incarceration for dealing with juveniles at a time when juvenile crime was declining nationally. The report showcased several departments in the nation, including Tarrant County, which went against the national trend with positive results. The report indicated Tarrant County's success was partly a result of deliberately keeping detention-space capacity small—the smallest capacity per capita of any of the seven largest urban counties in Texas—and relying, instead, on community services. "Neighboring counties have come to us and said, 'We don't have a lot of programs. Aren't they expensive?'" said Cockerell. "I tell them, we have more programming and less staff. I think they can do it, too. If their probation department looks at the funds and the way that they budget, they can do a lot more with what they have. The most expensive program—secure, institutional detention—is the one to develop last. If you develop the community-based programs first, you'll see which kids it will benefit and which kids it doesn't work for."[143]

Cockerell's leadership attracted international attention and provided a model for those across the pond to follow. Rotherham, England, entered into a partnership with Tarrant County early in 2001. In a Youth Services Bureau journal from June of that year, there is an article titled "Rotherham is doing it [juvenile justice] Texas style." Included in that article is Carey Cockerell's five-point plan for administering juvenile justice. The five-point plan was called "The American Way."

1. **Engage:** Young offenders are disengaged. They are separated and disenfranchised. They do not belong. It's our responsibility to bring them back instead of pushing them away.

2. **Speed:** Time to a juvenile is crucial. The quicker we can put a consequence to an action the quicker they can make the connection.

3. **Flexibility:** Services are categorical, and you always need other things that maybe you can't provide. If you can't deliver the service that is needed, go out and find it.

4. **Graduation:** We use the term graduated sanctions, which basically means making the punishment fit the crime. If a young person comes to you and doesn't need all the services, don't throw them all at him. You don't just give someone custody, because that's the whole load.

5. **Working Together:** This means everyone working with young people, be it education, health, social services, police, probation, mental health services, or whatever. Sometimes we all get in our little boxes and don't talk to each other. You are going to have to learn how the others do business and learn how you can do business together.[144]

During Mr. Cockerell's tenure, Tarrant County ushered in the first juvenile drug court in Texas. The drug court model originated in 1989 in Miami, Dade County, Florida. Abundant evidence suggests it is one of the most effective, if not *the* most effective, criminal justice program in the country. The first juvenile drug court began in 1993 in Florida, but Tarrant County boasts the first juvenile drug court in Texas. It is a unique preadjudication model that has been monitored and copied by other courts. It began operating in March 1999 and primarily serves young offenders who enter the system with substance-abuse issues.

All of these accomplishments brought widespread attention. Carey Cockerell's services began to be in demand. He was considered for the post of executive director of the Texas Youth Commission in the early 2000s, and in 2004, after twenty years of service to youth in Tarrant County, he was appointed executive director of the Texas Department of Family and Protective Services. Mr. Cockerell retired from service in Texas in 2008, seemingly for good. But in late August 2016, Mr. Cockerell's leadership was called upon again. Kentucky, managing its way through needed reform, tapped Mr. Cockerell to transform the system as the new commissioner for Kentucky's state department of juvenile justice.

The Maverick: Randy Turner

Is stability good or bad? It all depends on one's perspective. Stability by its very nature resists change, even when it might be necessary. But as US Army General Eric Shinseki once stated, according to Hesselbein & Goldsmith (2006), "If you don't like change, you're going to like irrelevance even less."[145] With more than three decades of working with young people, Randy Turner has been instrumental in bringing about that change. A stable, mature, and entrenched culture of doing things a certain way—with only three directors at the helm in almost sixty years—juvenile services came under the leadership of a director who likes to move, likes to keep moving forward, and likes to do that fast.

Chief Turner probably rubbed some people the wrong way in his historically brief time as director. He got off to a rocky start. Upon being named director, he told the entire staff at the first meeting: "If you do not like the vision, you can always leave." While there were likely a very few in the audience who had heard the same sort of admonition from Paul Cromwell in the 1970s, this confrontational approach had a similar effect on many of his staff, and it lingered the length of Turner's tenure. Randy Turner actually had a long career in the juvenile justice system as a whole, but limited time in community-based settings. Outside of serving as the chief of probation for five years in Oklahoma, most of his work had been in institutions. He was exposed to the philosophy of Tarrant County while serving as the director of the county's youth center and for one year as the department's assistant director in 2004. Yet he remained a maverick: definitely not afraid to shake things up to do what he believed was in the best interest of the kids in the system. He referenced Ron Corbett's definition of leadership as a telling part of his style:

> Leadership is poetry where management is prose. Leadership is tomorrow, not today—dreams not realities. "What if . . ." not "yes, but. . . ." Leadership means risk and danger, not safety and

security. It inspires; it does not mollify. . . .Leadership will scare you, worry you sick, infuriate you, make you crazy but never bore you. . . . It is a contact sport and when you win, you win big. It is the big dance.[146]

This is a bold definition of leadership. A maverick definition perhaps, and the fear, worry, and infuriation are felt by those who are led. Their responses are so *today*, and this kind of leader is focused on *tomorrow*. It takes some time for those two worlds to gel.

Leadership styles may be born or learned over time, but a maverick nature seems to be hardwired. If you look for Turner's mentor in leadership, look no further than his predecessor, Carey Cockerell. While they share much of the same philosophy, Turner is a man with a lot of his own ideas; to leave it at that, however, would only tell a part of the story. He enjoys processes and systems and adjusting these so they can work across a spectrum of situations. A hallmark of Turner's time in juvenile justice is that he adopted strategies based in empirical science—strategies that work. One of these was the establishment of a Quality Development Unit. He brought in a fulltime researcher to help the department navigate best practices and excellence in service delivery. It is now a staple of the juvenile justice movement at large.

Turner also sought to fully implement motivational interviewing in dealing with the juveniles in the system. Motivational interviewing is "a collaborative, goal-oriented method of communication with particular attention to the language of change. It is designed to strengthen an individual's motivation for and movement toward a specific goal by eliciting and exploring the person's own argument for change."[147] This approach is gaining ground across disciplines as an empathetic and collaborative approach to helping people achieve internal change. As with many such movements, its successful implementation in other disciplines is slowly influencing criminal and juvenile justice and leading to further reforms. During Turner's tenure, Tarrant County became the first juvenile probation system in Texas to support the development of a MINT (Motivational Interviewing Network of Trainers) member on its own staff, in an effort to fully implement the program and train its officers to respond to youth without relying on compliance and control. The hope is that the young person will develop an internal motivation toward change—a mindset that will persist well beyond the terms of probation.

Turner also advocated the use of technology and was diligent in applying technology as a tool to make systems more efficient and help officers be more productive. He helped the state usher in a twenty-first century internet-based case-management system, which is now utilized in all but four of the 254 Texas counties, with plans to be in all but one county by early 2019.

The proper assessment—the determination of a young person's needs and the risks inherent in his case—is quickly becoming one of the strongest components of evidence within juvenile justice. It is documented in risk, needs, and responsivity research. The basis of this research is that with limited resources, it is important to focus on those young people who have the greatest need and are most at risk of continuing on a path of delinquent conduct. The only way to make this determination is to have a thorough assessment process in place. Prior to Randy Turner's tenure, the depth of information collected on each young person was dependent upon the skill and dedication of the officer assigned to the case. Before Texas required such an assessment, Turner introduced a tool for a thorough and balanced assessment: the Positive Achievement Change Tool (PACT). The PACT provides a uniform approach for assessing juveniles across the spectrum. It looks at both risk and protective factors, produces results that can be measured, and provides the basis for generating a case plan based on criminogenic needs (those elements that, if addressed, might help a person avoid criminal activity)—resulting in an effective plan toward change.

The recent reform of the system at large, combined with the recession of the economy, has had a financial impact on the services available and on the number of people available to offer them. For the first time in the last half century, the program had to cut services, programs, and jobs, and as a result Randy Turner's leadership is marked almost as much for the programs that were lost as those that were added. Turner made the tough decision to bring an end to the following programs: separate intensive supervision caseloads; a post-adjudication program for those on intensive supervision who violated their terms; and, most recently, post-adjudication services for youth convicted of sexual offenses. Turner also made the decision to limit disruption for youth receiving services by not transferring youths to other officers, but by maintaining relationships between supervisors and their charges as the youths progressed through the system. The loss of funding and services had an emotional impact throughout the juvenile services organization, but Turner's necessary reorganization remained true to the county's historical principles by leveraging limited resources toward community-based programming rather than toward institutions.

Author Jon Gordon wrote the following about leadership: "People follow a leader first, and a vision second. The most optimistic person in the world can have the most inspiring vision, yet if the leader is not someone people will follow, the vision will not be realized."[148] Randy Turner articulated a compelling vision, a vision of reform. But leadership that sustains has multiple components. It involves the willingness of the organization to trust and follow the leader, a vision that is compelling to follow, and the commitment of the leader to retain good people. Randy Turner had the vision but struggled from the beginning with the people. On December 2, 2015, Turner announced his resignation from the department, stating that his "season" for service with the department was coming to a close; his resignation effective in April 2016.

The Relationship Builder: Bennie Medlin

Bennie Medlin became the director of the department on July 20, 2016. Mr. Medlin was the assistant director, later retitled deputy director, of the department in 2005 and served in that role for ten years under Director Turner. Medlin had known Turner from time in Dallas County early in his career. It is a testament to his ability to build relationships that a man seen by some as Turner's right-hand man could become the director after Turner's departure.

One of Medlin's elementary school friends lived with his grandmother, Ms. Marzell Hill. Marzell Hill was the first African American juvenile probation officer hired in Dallas County. Medlin stated that she often joked with him and his friend that she would take them to juvenile detention if they didn't act right. He wasn't always sure she was joking, but he was sure that he wanted to work in juvenile justice. Medlin went off to college to study psychology with a minor in law enforcement in order to come back to the metroplex and work in juvenile probation. He never forgot the impression that Marzell Hill had made on him. At some point, Medlin worked with other Dallas leaders to rename the Dallas county transition shelter for nondelinquent youth after the woman who had inspired him.[149]

Arriving back in Dallas in 1981, the first opportunity to get involved was as a part-time detention officer. Medlin quickly got several opportunities to promote in his work in detention. He felt like he could influence more juveniles by passing on what he had learned to other officers. Medlin indicated that he has been a lifelong learner, and that growing meant taking on new opportunities.

Taking on some responsibilities and advancing further would mean leaving the place he always wanted to be: the Dallas area. Twice in his career, Medlin left Texas for Florida, once working for Florida's state juvenile justice system, and another time for a private contractor. Each time it meant taking on greater responsibility and learning new things. It was also always with the intention of coming back to the metroplex, after learning and being in situations that would help him receive opportunities to expand his influence.

Bennie Medlin always believed that would be a return to Dallas, but the opportunity ended up being in nearby Tarrant County. A one-time colleague, Richard Neddlekoff, had reached out from Florida to prompt each of Medlin's departures from the metroplex. Neddlekoff himself was a dedicated public servant, and a very politically connected individual. Neddlekoff spent time in Washington DC as the director of the Bureau of Justice and as the executive director of Criminal Justice in Texas. He also had stints as a regional director for Florida's juvenile justice system, and was a chief executive over a few large private and non-profit services in the state. A former aide to George W. Bush, he was also appointed conservator of the Texas Youth Commission by Rick Perry in late 2007. Arriving back in Texas prior to Bennie, Neddlekoff called Medlin in 2005 to let him know that Tarrant County needed an assistant director and asked him if he knew the Director, Randy Turner. It didn't take long for Medlin to submit an application online and then call Turner to let him know of his interest. He became the assistant director of Tarrant County in July 2005.

Bennie Medlin referred to his time as the assistant director, and then later deputy director, as a lesson in leadership. A somewhat turbulent time allowed Mr. Medlin to reflect on his own style of leadership, affirming that his style was something that people responded to while learning, if given the chance, what not to do. Mostly, it affirmed that to do the work of juvenile justice—or to truly lead in any field, for that matter—being effective meant building and nurturing relationships. Medlin recognized that the relationships Turner established outside the agency were important but also learned it was important to build them inside the agency. He describes his approach as being flexible and being a situational leader. This allows a leader to understand and meet people where they are, and offers an opportunity to help them develop. Earlier in his career, he also learned the importance of a mission and a vision if one is to be the north star for an agency.

Medlin's philosophy of juvenile justice is generally about creating an environment where young people can thrive and understanding the barriers that get in the way of such an environment. He credits his experience and his recent education—a master's degree in criminal justice from the University of Texas at Arlington—with helping him evolve as a learner as the system evolves. He credits his return to school with helping him understand more clearly the importance of research and the evidence of what works in further understanding what helps young people thrive.

Bennie Medlin knew from an early age that he wanted to be a juvenile probation officer. The irony is that he never had that title until his recent appointment as the director. For the most part he had worked in institutional settings prior to his tenure in Tarrant County. Medlin stated that his father is his mentor. His father worked two jobs. In addition to a strong work ethic, his father knew everybody in the neighborhood. Bennie Medlin feels that those attributes were passed on to him, along with the desire to get an education so that he could be more available to his family. It really is all about relationships.

FIVE

The Bench

From its inception in the early twentieth century, County Judge John Terrell was probably the most invested and the biggest believer in the ideals of the juvenile court. As county judge, Terrell dealt with county matters in the boom time of Tarrant County. His loyalty, by definition, was divided, but that was never apparent. The time he was able to give to the juvenile court was out of an overflow of passion for the dream. The juvenile court, for those who work in it, is more akin to a calling than to a job or profession. The shifting winds of politics can be just as devastating to those in elected office as they are to juvenile justice itself. Judge John Terrell felt the sting of political will when he was voted out of office in 1910.

His departure from office nearly killed the juvenile court. During his time and even after, he had been the advocate, the marketer, the nurturer, the judge. In his short three years as the leader of the Juvenile Court of Tarrant County, he had brought national attention to the work of his court, his probation officer, and the dream of juvenile justice. During that time, he brought both the controversial juvenile judge of Denver, Ben Lindsey, and the father of the juvenile court, Dr. A. S. Orse of Chicago, to the city of Fort Worth to talk about the dream of juvenile justice. Without Terrell's leadership, that dream almost died, and the heart of the juvenile court in Tarrant County stopped beating.[150]

It would be hard to argue the value of his leadership. How could the county move forward without it? The court was resuscitated, however, after a brief coma and continued to do good work. As has often been the case in juvenile justice, its mission is at times relegated to second-class status. It would not take long and would only require the interview of the nation's schoolteachers to learn that our country still deals with the struggle between *property* and *priority* when it comes to kids. We talk about their importance, their value, but it rarely looks that way on the bottom line. Juvenile justice was at the same disadvantage, at least in the early days. There was typically a rotating judge. No one judge performed the bulk of the work, and for many justices, it was a sideline to their real assignment, a distraction. Once election time came and went, a new judge would be tasked with learning this part-time role. Unless it became a passion, it is hard to see why these judges would invest much time in such study.

In 1943, a law was passed that created a juvenile board. The law stated that the body of district judges within a county would be responsible for the local oversight and guidance of the juvenile court. Slowly but surely, the juvenile court was accorded the smallest of platforms where its work might remain front and center.[151]

In 1962, Tarrant County created the Domestic Relations Court with a judge to oversee all matters related to the welfare of families and children. Judge Eva Barnes was appointed to this bench. She had been the first female assistant district attorney in Tarrant County under the leadership of District Attorney Tim Curry. In her new position Judge Barnes began to handle juvenile matters as a part of her function.[152]

In 1965, a second Domestic Relations Court was created, and a new appointment was to be made. Texas Governor John Connally Jr. had a tough decision and likely depended on a small voice within the state house to help him finally make it. Politicians always want to look smart and seek to make sound decisions, but the one influenced by Don Kennard would be a bedrock decision.[153]

Don Kennard was elected to the House of Representatives in 1962. While never working a delinquency case, and never really understanding its nuances, he had a tremendous impact on Tarrant County Juvenile Services, the state of Texas, and the dream of juvenile justice.[154]

Don was thirteen years old when he moved to Fort Worth with his family. He soon became a student at Arlington Heights High School. It turns out he was a decent football player and became fast friends with a kid others called "Bunny" because he had unusually white hair for an adolescent. The towheaded kid's name was Scott Dean Moore, and he also played football as well as basketball for the Yellow Jackets. The two remained close as they both chose to attend the University of Texas, where Scott earned a degree in business administration in 1951.[155]

Scott's lifelong ambition was to be a lawyer, and he went on to law school at the University of Texas. He graduated in 1954. Following military service in Japan, he returned to Fort Worth in 1956, where he took a position as assistant district attorney. He left the DA's office in 1959 to enter private practice.

In 1965, when the governor was deciding who should take the court working with children in Fort Worth, Representative Don Kennard had one name for him: Scott Moore.[156]

Governor Connally listened, and Scott Moore went to work alongside Eva Barnes. Assigned to Domestic Relations Court #2, he held court over child welfare, family law, and juvenile delinquency matters on the third floor of the Tarrant County Civil Courthouse. This would have a major impact on the Juvenile Court.[157]

In 1967, the legislature passed a law creating a third Domestic Relations Court, and thus an opportunity for Tarrant County Juvenile Services. The decision was made to have one of the Domestic Relations Courts be set apart as the juvenile court for the county. There was clearly a judge with a passion for the position. In 1967, the juvenile board of Tarrant County, of which Moore was a member, met to make the determination of who might take that position. With Scott and Eva in the room, the board asked them if they wanted to leave so they could appropriately talk about them behind their backs. Both Eva and Judge Moore, who often appreciated a man or woman who would just shoot straight with him, declined the request to leave, and a discussion ensued that would result in Scott D. Moore becoming the juvenile court judge of Tarrant County on September 1, 1967. The court was separate and distinct from the traditional domestic relations courts, and Moore would have sole responsibility for it along with other matters involving the welfare of children.[158]

Like Kennard's nod and Connally's appointment, the selection of the juvenile board was another step toward the swift yet steady rise of this giant in the profession. Scott Moore shared something with his partner, Lynn Ross, in juvenile justice in Tarrant County. He had presence, and people recognized it from the first time they came into contact with him. It was an almost perfect partnership, and such a rarity to have two leaders of this magnitude. They shared something else: longevity. Together their leadership was a stable force that strengthened juvenile justice in Tarrant County for decades. Judge Moore served for over three decades (including his time as visiting retired judge)—unheard of for an elected official.

Judge Moore's only real experience with juveniles was raising a home full of children (five), but that alone seems to have been all he needed. Tarrant County once again had a leader on the bench with a passion for doing what was right for young people. Judge Terrell must have been smiling from above. Judge Moore would restore passionate purpose to juvenile services in Tarrant County, making it a model of good practice both statewide and nationally. Unlike Terrell, he would have the opportunity to nurture the dream to fruition. Carey Cockerell described him in this way: "Judge Moore was a Democrat, and that meant something to him. He believed in the underdog. He believed in these kids."[159]

Judge Moore was instrumental in establishing a Child Protective Services (CPS) unit to address the needs of abused and neglected children in Tarrant County. He supported efforts that led to the founding of Court-Appointed Special Advocates (CASA) and supported A. Smith Gill Children's services, a foundation to help children in financial need, particularly where there were gaps in services.[160]

In addition to taking many local leadership roles, Judge Moore was appointed chair of the Juvenile Court Judges Division of the State Bar of Texas by the governor and served on the Texas Juvenile Probation Commission. Along with Bob Dawson, he provided leadership in the work of the Texas House of Representatives in the landmark 1973 writing of the Texas Family Code, which codified family and juvenile justice law in Texas.[161]

Judge Moore was also appointed to the House Investigating Committee looking into abuses at TYC in 1969. He was one of the "midnight raiders" who showed up unannounced at the Gatesville State Schools to investigate the claims of abuse in the system. He was part of the group that questioned some of the boys and reported that some of them appeared to have been physically beaten with something other than fists. This group also heard testimony in Austin indicating these young people had been terrorized and beaten.[162]

Judge Moore was known by many as a very generous and caring man, but he also had a reputation for being a very stern jurist. There were two things he did not tolerate from the attorneys, officers, and others who worked in his court: laziness and untruthfulness. He would not accept anything other than someone's best. In order to do what was in the best interest of the child, you had to be prepared. He wouldn't accept "I don't know." He didn't want staff to act as if they had done their best if they hadn't or to make excuses about why they weren't prepared. This led to some being anxious in his court, but usually it meant that his officers came to work fully prepared and bringing their best.[163]

One of the distinctive features of the Juvenile Court in Tarrant County under Judge Moore's leadership was the three-day rule. This rule was his creation and an effort to expedite juvenile cases where the young person was waiting in detention or in the county jail for a court date. Moore believed that a young person should not spend an inordinate amount of time awaiting a hearing. The real purpose of the juvenile court was rehabilitation, and that could only happen after the disposition of the case.[164]

Detention was designed, from the beginning of juvenile law in Texas, as a place for a young person to await adjudication. It was not designed as a "shock" to the system to help a young person make better decisions. It was designed to ensure that someone would appear for court. Its use has expanded to provide for public safety and to shelter juveniles in cases where suitable supervision was not available without intervention in the home.

The three-day rule curtailed the amount of time the District Attorney's Office would be given by the court to file a petition for a young person in custody. In a world where the speed of the docket is paramount based upon the right to a speedy trial, this is light speed, even for juvenile justice. It is unique in the justice system, and at times has created conflict between the court and the Tarrant County DA's office. Judge Moore was interested in one thing, and that was the best interest of children. There has since been federal legislation limiting detention times for juveniles, and evidence suggesting that long-term detention has adverse effects on young people. In many ways, based on intuition and trial and error, Judge Moore's ruling was evidence-based before there was such a notion.[165]

Judge Moore's belief in a speedy docket, his principles regarding the way detention should be used, and his commitment to a low per-capita commitment rate to the state schools came from a unique perspective. He was involved in a committee appointed by the governor to look into allegations of abuse in the state schools and was involved in a long campaign to remove young people from the county jail. A 1969 article in the *Dallas Morning News* discussed his reduction in commitments to the state school, and he was asked if it was due to his involvement on the committee. He said no and indicated wisely that it was the result of having more probation officers who could provide appropriate supervision and guidance in the community. Truth be told, there is more than an outside chance that additional officers were hired specifically in order to avoid sending young people to the state schools.[166]

Judge Moore received numerous awards and honors during his tenure over the 323rd District Court. He was named Citizen of the Year in 1979 by the Texas chapter of the National Association of Social Workers. He was selected by the United Way to receive the Hercules Award, exemplifying his outstanding human service in the community. In 1993, Judge Moore was named to the Hall of Honor by the Texas Corrections Association for outstanding public service. The National Council of Juvenile and Family Court Judges bestowed a lifetime achievement award on him in 1992, when he received the council's highest award for Meritorious Service to the Juvenile Courts of America.[167]

Judge Ernie Bates

Ernie Bates became the first associate judge in Judge Moore's court, with the title of court master. Bates served in this role until appointed to the 297th District Court in 1986. Bates has practiced law since 1974. He has been a prominent defense attorney in Tarrant County since leaving the bench in 1990 and continues to practice law, including juvenile law.[168]

Judge Jean Hudson Boyd

Judge Boyd was only the second full-time Juvenile Court Judge of the 323rd District Court of Tarrant County—the juvenile court. She was elected to the bench after her mentor, Judge Moore, retired in 1994. She served on the juvenile court bench in some capacity for twenty-eight years and served Tarrant County as a public servant for thirty-three years. Judge Boyd retired from the bench in December 2014.

Jean Boyd began her career as assistant district attorney for Tarrant County. What some might call an accident, others might call destiny. Her father was a lawyer, as her great-grandfather had been. Originally, Jean Boyd wanted to be a scientist or a teacher. She was a science major who liked both science and math when she entered college at Texas Tech. Her college adviser steered her away from math, however, so she focused on zoology and chemistry. She had plans to go to graduate school at Tech with a science major.[169]

Judge Boyd's plans changed after college, as she prepared to move to Houston with her husband. Her landlord refused to return her security deposit, and she wanted to take appropriate legal action. Her husband shared her indignation, but told her, "Honey, no attorney will take this for that amount of money." Jean Boyd felt there was a principle to defend, however. She was a college student, and if they would take advantage of her, they would take advantage of others. She called her father and eventually got her deposit back.[170]

In Houston, Boyd considered getting a teaching certificate in science but learned that it would take her almost three years to obtain it. She discovered that she could finish law school in the same amount of time. Armed with that information, she took the Law School Admissions Test (LSAT). She applied to two schools: the University of Houston and South Texas School of Law. She would have to wait a year to enter the University of Houston. She called South Texas, and they invited her for a visit with the dean. She attended orientation the next day, attended law school from 1978 to 1979, and was licensed in May of 1979 to practice law in Texas.[171]

Jean Boyd's first job as a lawyer was in Houston with ETPM, an offshore oil construction business. When ETPM closed down, she moved to Fort Worth. Her husband was finishing dental school with a practicum in the metroplex. Jean Boyd was the sole provider of income and was looking for work. She applied with the Tarrant County District Attorney's Office. She did not get the job on her first, second, or third application. She eventually got a job with the Fort Worth City Attorney's Office. She kept her options open and had coffee once a month with a supervisor in the District Attorney's Office. The fourth time a job came open, she was hired in the civil division of the child support enforcement division of the DA's office.[172]

After a short time in the office, she took maternity leave for the birth of her son. She came back and realized that at that time, the office didn't really know what to do with women. She was one of a very few in their employ. She started another position in the DA's office, working with Child Protective Services. Not long after, every other person (every male) received raises, but she did not. Boyd visited District Attorney Tim Curry, and she got her raise. She worked in the CPS division at the corner of Riverside Drive and Berry Street, and with a son at home, the work of protecting children took on new meaning. She was happy with her role.[173]

A chance encounter might describe her first meeting with Judge Moore. The bailiff of her court informed her division that a district attorney hadn't shown up in another family court. Her supervisor told Boyd that a judge was furious, and quickly sent her to stand in. With a map drawn by the supervisor, and a copy of the family code,

Jean Boyd rushed to this unfamiliar court. When she arrived, the CPS worker filled her in on the details: a child had been abused and had a retinal hemorrhage as a result. Apparently Boyd looked like a fish out of water; the bailiff asked her three times if she was an attorney. "If I couldn't convince a bailiff, how was I going to get through this?" Boyd recalled. Apparently, she was able to convince a furious Judge Moore, for he informed her of a position with the DA's office that was open in his court; it involved taking over most juvenile and CPS cases. Judge Boyd remembered it being a great experience, even though it was a "trial by fire." During the afternoons she worked with Judge Moore to set up procedures and schedules for reviewing ongoing cases and removing children from abusive situations; it took her most mornings to type up and sort out the necessary reports and paperwork.[174]

It wasn't long after her time in Judge Moore's court that Ernie Bates was appointed to a district criminal court after the incumbent had passed away unexpectedly. His position as associate judge in the juvenile court became available. At this point, Boyd had been pondering a move. She had been with the DA's office six years, and although she had assumed she would be a career prosecutor, she hadn't been interested in the positions that had opened up in that office. Judge Scott Moore asked Jean Boyd to consider putting in an application for the associate judge position. Boyd had a young child and thought a more stable job with regular office hours would be beneficial. There would be a large number of applicants for the juvenile court position, however. Boyd thought little of her chances, but she decided it wouldn't hurt to try.[175]

Others had even less confidence in her chances. The other attorneys as much as told her she would never get the judgeship, partly because she was green, but mostly because she was a woman. Boyd continued to work as a prosecutor in Judge Moore's court, and noticed that all of the attorneys (all male) had been interviewing for the position. Judge Moore eventually acknowledged that he wasn't planning to interview her. He stated that they had been working closely together, and that he knew how she would answer just about all of the questions he would ask. Boyd went home that afternoon and told her husband that she didn't get the job.[176]

She was mistaken. In February of 1987, Jean Boyd became the associate judge of the 323rd District Court. The first week on the job involved observing Judge Moore in action. Jean Boyd was an associate judge from 1987 to 1995. In October of 1994, Judge Moore announced his retirement after nearly thirty years on the bench. It was an unexpected announcement and a "big shock" to Judge Boyd. A bigger shock remained: he asked her if she would seek the bench.[177]

Jean Boyd stated that being on the bench as an associate was a great opportunity for her to learn and to have the kind of career stability she wanted as a woman with a family. She had never been politically ambitious, and the thought of campaigning for office did not appeal to her. But her concern for the children and families she served quickly overrode her doubts. Who might get the bench if she did not run? Would he have a different philosophy for children? How would he run the docket? What kind of ethical values would he hold? Would he be concerned with expediting cases for the right reasons?[178]

Judge Boyd ran successfully against Marshall Hines, then an assistant district attorney, and Robert Cortez. Her dislike for the campaign trail did not turn out to be much of a problem: She would only have one other contested race during her tenure, a race against Assistant District Attorney Sean Colston in 1998.[179]

Scott Moore had been in charge of the newly formed Juvenile Justice Committee of the judicial section of the state bar and held meetings in Fort Worth that at times included Bob Dawson. This event grew into an annual conference that hosted its 28th version in Fort Worth in 2015. This conference continues to meet on a rotating basis throughout the state. Toward the end of Judge Moore's tenure, Judge Boyd was encouraged to take on this event. She was the chair-elect for the juvenile section of the state bar during 1993 and 1994. In 1995, after just a few weeks on the bench, Judge Boyd received a call asking if she would assume Scott Moore's position as the chair of the Juvenile Justice Committee of the judicial section of the state bar, a position Judge Moore had held during most of his time on the bench.[180]

As an associate judge, Boyd had the opportunity to work alongside Judge Timothy Menikos when Judge Moore appointed Menikos as a second associate in 1992. Once she was elected to the bench, Boyd hired Ellen Smith to take her place. In 2000, with a growing population and an expanding docket, Boyd hired a third associate judge, Kim Brown.[181]

Child welfare experience was cited by Judge Boyd as something she really looked for in an associate for the 323rd District Court, and she maintained Judge Moore did the same. Boyd stated that close to half of all juvenile justice cases likely have a child welfare component to them—whether they were referred or assessed or not. This number grows when it involves a commitment to the Texas Juvenile

Justice Department (the institutional component of the juvenile justice system), according to the judge. "If you can decide whether or not a child should be removed from their parents, you can make all of the other decisions needed in juvenile justice," she maintains. Judge Boyd felt CPS cases required the most difficult decisions a judge could make. Before coming to the bench, Judge Menikos and Smith had experience with both CPS and child welfare, while Judge Boyd and Judge Kim Brown primarily had child welfare experience.[182]

Judge Boyd instituted Monday morning meetings for her and the three associates, in part to study for board certification as certified Juvenile Law Specialists. Boyd and the three associates took the first exam offered, making Tarrant County the first multi-judge juvenile court jurisdiction to have the entire bench certified as specialists. After the exam, the judges continued their weekly meetings for consistency, pursuing a team approach. Being a judge can be very lonely, Boyd points out, and supporting each other and the decisions each hands down is important to continuity and morale.[183]

Judge Boyd remembers the direction of juvenile justice in the past with some fondness but is not entirely optimistic about its future. A big part of the movement's past success was Bob Dawson, the professor from UT responsible for writing the Juvenile Justice Code. Dawson explained things in certain ways to the legislature, and more importantly would stand up to the legislature when needed—and they would listen. One example offered by Judge Boyd is the concept of mandatory sex offender registration. In the first pass, all juveniles with a sexual offense—one that could involve a broad range of circumstances—were treated the same. Dawson was able to revise the law to allow for judicial discretion. Dawson was something of a "lawyer whisperer." He could take reasoned arguments from the field—from judges, defense lawyers, probation officers, prosecutors—and make sense of it all to the legislature in a way that generally pleased the entire field. That is no small task. Judge Boyd said you could call Dawson directly and that he would often call to ask questions or solicit comments about a law or a given scenario. There is a void at the state level, she said, ever since Dawson passed away.[184]

Judge Boyd expressed concern about the direction of the newly created Texas state juvenile agency, the Texas Juvenile Justice Department. In 2018, just seven years after the creation of TJJD, it has seen four appointed directors plus several interims. There has been some push and pull between the facilities model and a more rehabilitative philosophy. Judge Boyd is concerned about the stability of a system that sees a parade of new administrators and new ideas that may reflect the politics of the times more than they do a depth of understanding or familiarity with the history of juvenile justice.[185]

Just as it did with Scott Moore, the 323rd District Court received recognition during Boyd's time on the bench. She became the first woman to receive the Silver Gavel Award in 2011 from the Tarrant County Bar Association. This award is for jurists who have been on the bench for over ten years and exemplify ability, integrity, and courage.[186]

Scott Moore, Boyd maintains, was visionary in his leadership. He created the three-day rule in order to control the docket and the size of the population in the small juvenile detention center. "How did he think of that?" she has asked in amazement. How did he know that it would be allowed in the law, much less accepted by the attorneys and prosecutors impacted by it?[187]

The philosophy of working with juveniles, as Boyd describes it, is boldly simple. The life of a juvenile can be turned around, and science, with its understanding of adolescent brain development, has something to say about how that is achieved. With higher brain functions such as impulse control still in developmental stages, juveniles can easily make mistakes that will have a lifelong negative impact. Appropriate supervision is key. Boyd believes in the Texas mandate that children should be kept in their community and with family whenever possible, with work toward developing new behaviors. Boyd believes in providing services as quickly as possible, which necessitates a speedy docket. Delayed services are less effective services. These principles, Boyd said, are simply borrowed from her predecessor, Scott Moore. "He knew that the more often attorneys are asked to be present for court, the more likely it would be that something could get resolved."[188] But to suggest it was simple to follow such a bold and sure vision would not give Judge Boyd enough credit. Standing behind that mandate required a thick skin.

Judge Timothy A. Menikos

"Tim, I think you would be a good judge" were the words spoken to Judge Menikos by the most important man in his life—his father. Menikos remembers with vivid clarity a lunch he had with his father when he was seventeen. Menikos was attending Arlington Heights High School—the school Scott Moore had attended before him—and was a junior who would graduate early. He wasn't sure what to do with himself, but his father's words rang true.

In 1992, Judge Moore appointed Timothy Menikos associate judge for the 323rd District Court. Menikos was sworn in as the court's third full-time judge on January 9, 2015. His late father would have been proud.

Judge Menikos completed his undergraduate degree at North Texas State in Denton. He had been to classes at Tarrant County Junior College and the University of Texas in Austin. There was no prelaw, so he settled on banking and finance. He completed law school at St. Mary's and Texas Tech.[189]

He began his legal career in 1985. He was in private practice with George Kredell until Kredell accepted an appointment as a district judge in 1988. Menikos worked a number of cases but particularly liked working juvenile and family law. The words of his father haunted him a bit at first. Menikos threw his hat in the ring for several judicial positions. He applied for the spot that Judge Moore gave to Ernie Bates. He applied again when Bates left, losing the spot to Judge Boyd. He tried for a Justice of the Peace position. He eventually began to think there had to be another path and took a position as the attorney for an insurance firm in 1990. After about a year and a half, he reopened a solo private practice. Half of his cases were juvenile and CPS cases in the 323rd District Court.[190]

It wasn't long after Menikos reopened his private practice that Ernie Bates took a position with another district court, and the second associate bench spot opened up. When the opening was announced, several probation officers reached out to Timothy Menikos to let him know there was an opportunity to return to the juvenile court. They knew the kind of attorney he was: a confirmed advocate for the best interests of young people.[191]

Judge Menikos's early memories of Judge Scott Moore were that everyone was afraid of the man. Judge Menikos wasn't sure why, as he found him warm and funny. He did notice that Judge Moore got real joy out of "jerking people's chains." "He treated me like a nephew—with the utmost respect," Menikos remembered, but he recognized early on that Judge Moore was "not to be messed with." It took Menikos a while to realize Moore even had a first name, as he only knew him as Judge Moore.[192]

There was a family feeling around the department, and most of the attorneys were old running buddies of Judge Moore. They were his contemporaries. Either you knew Judge Moore as a peer, as they did, and had that ease and comfort with him, or you knew him by reputation. Judge Menikos, who was younger than Moore and the others, said he "would have never guessed [Moore] would think I would be a better candidate" than others who put in for the position.[193]

Nonetheless, in 1992, Judge Menikos was appointed an associate judge in Judge Moore's court. Originally, his quarters were in what is now the district clerk's station. He had a ten-by-twelve-foot office with a single table, four chairs, and a door. There was a tape recorder but no bailiff. A courtroom was eventually squeezed out of some space facing the old detention center. Judge Menikos wasn't too proud to serve in those undersized settings. He told Judge Moore, when he offered him the position, that he "appreciated the trust, and would give it my all." Judge Moore dryly replied, "I know that Tim—it is why I picked you."[194]

"He was always the boss with me," Menikos recalled. Judge Moore could be very different and loose at conference settings but was all work at the courthouse. He made that very clear to Judge Menikos and the other associates. A judge is always judicial. A judge is conscious of the way he or she looks and acts in the courtroom. "Never take the bench in shirtsleeves," Judge Moore told him. "Never wear anything other than a white shirt and a suit." The image of a judge was important.[195]

In late 1994, Judge Menikos was just as shocked as everyone else when Judge Moore decided to retire. Menikos could hear his father's refrain and gave some thought to whether or not he should run. He then learned from Judge Moore that he was asking Judge Boyd to run. Would he please his father or Judge Moore in his decision? Menikos remembered that Scott Moore always had the associate judges' backs, and it was important for him that all of his associates present a united front. Judge Menikos lined up behind Moore and offered his support to Judge Boyd. Maybe his father had meant that he would make a good associate judge. There was no shame in that.[196]

When Judge Boyd won the election, the stability and continuity of the 323rd District Court was assured, and Judge Menikos would be a part of that legacy. He was now an associate judge who had served under both the first and the second juvenile judges ever to serve Tarrant County. He would also move up to a full-size courtroom.

Following the pattern of continuity established by Scott Moore, Judge Menikos got the chance he hoped for in 2014, when Judge Boyd made the decision to retire. Judge Menikos won the subsequent election, and the legacy continued.

Judge Ellen Smith

Ellen Smith was appointed an associate judge in the 323rd District Court in 1995 by Judge Boyd. Smith started practicing family law with a firm that covered other cases. Attorney Bob Hoover was a partner in the firm and was practicing some family law. He decided to mentor Smith and introduced her to Judge Moore and the department. Since family law was not bringing in a lot of money for the firm, the partners decided that the new attorney could handle that work.[197]

Ellen Smith got on the appointment list to work in Moore's court. At that time there was no predetermined rotation list. Judge Moore decided who would be appointed based on his personal knowledge of an attorney and the kind of dedication he or she showed with young people. If you worked hard and cared about kids, Judge Moore would put you on the rotation. At this time Texas Wesleyan Law School did not exist, so there was only a small group of dedicated local attorneys available for the work. That small pool provided a level of camaraderie that is hard to find in recent times. Judge Moore loved having people he knew around to share stories, and this engendered a family feel among the attorneys who worked in his court.[198]

In 1992, Ellen Smith went into private practice with Ellen Tyler, Judge Moore's daughter. This was around the time that the associate judgeship awarded to Timothy Menikos had become available. Smith remembers thinking about applying at that time but acted on the advice she received from another jurist: "You're never a real lawyer until you hang your own shingle." Ellen Smith enjoyed the independence and freedom she found in private practice but didn't hesitate long when another courtroom was opened in the 323rd District Court.[199]

Sharon Fuller, a juvenile court clerk who worked both for Judge Moore and Judge Boyd, remembers getting Smith's application and telling Judge Boyd, "I'm not sure we need to keep looking. Ellen has applied." Sharon simply knew that Ellen Smith was passionate about her work with young people.[200]

Judge Smith began work as Judge Boyd's second associate judge in 1995. At that time, as a retired district judge, Judge Moore occasionally came in to hear cases in Judge Boyd's or an associate judge's absence. Judge Smith remembered often going in to talk to him about cases, and particularly remembers being upset about the tension she felt among attorneys when she made rulings they didn't like. Smith told Judge Moore she was pretty sure that no one (defense attorneys or prosecutors) was very happy with her. "You're doing something right, if no one is really satisfied," Judge Moore told her. "He was gruff to some folks," Smith remembers, "but never with the kids."[201]

Judge Smith also remembered a "golden age" in juvenile work when Toby Goodman and Robert Dawson were working with the legislature. It was a golden age because Goodman and Dawson wanted to hear from the field. She remembered being able to communicate directly with Dawson about concerns with the law, and "he would make things happen almost immediately."[202]

Judge Smith has continued in the tradition of making things happen from the bench. In 2008, she became the judge for a Family Drug Court model in working with addicted mothers. In an effort to reunite birth mothers with their infant children, this court used an evidence-based model to help addicted mothers and hold them accountable in getting clean.

Judge Kim Brown

Kim Brown was appointed the third associate judge of the 323rd District Court in 1999 by Judge Boyd. Brown had served as assistant district attorney with Child Protective Services. Until recently, Judge Brown had been the "rookie" of the court, despite having served almost two decades on the bench.

Kim Brown grew up in Richardson, Texas. She decided to pursue a career in music after seeing a Dallas summer musical in high school.[203] She went to Texas Tech to pursue that dream, but her plans changed after graduating and staying in Lubbock. She went to law school at Texas Tech before taking a job in child support enforcement with the attorney general's office in Fort Worth. She then took a job as a prosecutor for Tarrant County in CPS from 1992 to 1999, working the latter part of those years primarily in the 323rd District Court. Her decision to apply for the position in Judge Boyd's court was prompted largely by a rise in the number of CPS cases she was prosecuting. As a mother herself, she had empathy for the children and the parents.[204]

Judge James Teel

James Teel became the most recent addition to the 323rd District Court when Judge Menikos was elected to the bench and appointed Teel an associate judge in 2015. Judge Teel knew in high school that he wanted to practice law. He grew up in Haltom City and graduated from Haltom High School. His father, a lawyer, was his inspiration for pursuing law, and he graduated from law school at Texas Tech knowing he wanted to return to the metroplex. Judge Teel's law career started as a prosecutor in Tarrant County's criminal division. To advance your career as a felony prosecutor meant passing through juvenile. Judge Teel remembered, like most other prosecutors, fearing appointment to juvenile court. It was a rite of passage, and most attorneys dreaded the ritual. A lawyer just needed to bide their time, get some experience working felony cases, and then they could return downtown to practice real law. Judge Teel planned on taking that route, but he fell in love with the intricacies and the differences evident early on in working juvenile justice. Judge Teel's time as a prosecutor in juvenile court began in the 80s when Judge Scott Moore was still on the bench. Not long after transferring back downtown, Judge Teel branched out on his own to become a criminal defense attorney. He set up his private practice across the street from the juvenile justice center, with intent to have a large portion of his practice in juvenile justice. Judge Moore specifically reached out to Judge Teel to also take child welfare appointments. Judge Teel stated, "You didn't say no to Judge Moore."[205] Judge Teel appreciated that in juvenile justice, it was a collaborative approach. An attorney needed to know about the system, and the people needed to know and work with the opposing counsel to help young people and families. Judge Teel worked in private practice for ten years. He put his name in for consideration when Judge Brown was appointed, and after not getting the position, became the chief prosecutor for the Child Welfare division. This continued his work in the juvenile court, and when Judge Menikos became the district judge, Judge Teel was appointed to the bench.

A New Chapter

Judge Menikos will retire in 2018. In November 2018, Tarrant County will elect its third full-time judge of the 323rd District Court. Whoever is elected will be the first judge that did not serve as a judge under Judge Scott Moore. James Teel has been nominated by the Democratic party, Alex Kim by the Republicans. Although he was not a judge, Teel did work extensively in Judge Moore's court as a lawyer. Kim handled juvenile cases earlier in his career but has had limited recent experience in juvenile or child welfare cases. Regardless of the outcome of the election, the threads of continuity will be forever altered.

SIX

The Juvenile Justice Code

In 1973, more than six decades after the inception of its juvenile court, the State of Texas made its first real attempt to draft a specific code to guide juvenile justice. Prior to that time there were ephemeral laws but no uniformity. The 1973 code, written by Bob Dawson with the counsel of Scott Moore and others, was good work, but it was insufficient to guide a system that had been seeking guidance for over sixty years.[206]

In 1995, this more complete picture of what juvenile justice should look like was finally codified into law in the face of a number of factors: rising juvenile crime, rising violent crime, and alarm at the national level over a wave of unprecedented youth violence. Criminologist John Dilulio coined the term "super predator" in 1992, on the assumption that the moral deficiency of the country's youth had hit an all-time low. This led to "get tough" legislation in Texas, among other places. All of this had a major impact on the blending of adult and juvenile justice practices, swinging the pendulum back toward the use of incarceration.[207]

Toby Goodman
Toby Goodman was born in Archer City, Texas, and after a college athletic career at Texas Christian University and an all-expenses-paid stay in Southeast Asia (via the military), he returned to Tarrant County to begin his law career. Getting into local politics led Goodman to run for state representative for the area and, without his realizing it, led a man who had never tried a delinquency case to be the architect of a very successful Juvenile Justice Code. Goodman was an expert not in only juvenile law but in what worked for young people in need.[208]

State Representative Toby Goodman of Arlington very quickly learned about the work of Tarrant County and its reputation as a model for other courts. Along with UT professor Bob Dawson, he is responsible for Texas's comprehensive juvenile justice code. He is very proud of the fact that while several pieces of Title 3 have been challenged, not a single line has been successfully appealed. He attributes this to the careful attention of Robert Dawson.[209]

"[Dawson] is probably the single most important factor in the lives of children in Texas," said Goodman, who shepherded the state's juvenile justice code revision through the legislature in 1995. "The Juvenile Code in Texas is patterned across the nation. This created a comprehensive juvenile system, addressing causes and prevention, not just punishment. He's the mastermind. Any legislation I carried, he wrote."[210]

"Bob came in and essentially walked me through the whole juvenile process," Goodman said. The result—House Bill 327—was what Goodman calls "the first comprehensive approach to handling juvenile offenders in the United States, incorporating set sentencing and progressive sentencing options, prevention and intervention programs to keep kids out of the adult criminal system or get them help for mental problems, and rehabilitation programs to educate and train young offenders before they are released."[211]

"Since the 1995 comprehensive revision in juvenile law, juvenile crime has gone down every year, by almost 20 percent through 2003, despite close to a 20 percent rise in the state's juvenile population during the same time. The number of repeat offenders is down, and dramatically fewer juvenile offenders are prosecuted as adults."[212]

Goodman was eventually asked to assist then governor George Bush in writing his campaign plan for juvenile justice. Governor Bush signed the 1995 legislation in Arlington, in a nod to Toby Goodman's work in getting the legislation through. Goodman is still active in politics and is sought in lobbying efforts, most recently for the Juvenile Justice Association of Texas.[213]

Robert Dawson

There are some people who gain fame by being known by one name. It probably started with Madonna, although Napoleon might have something to say about the phenomenon, or maybe even Prince, before he was the artist formerly known as Prince.

In Texas Juvenile Justice, Dawson has such status. You can say the first name, but only the last is needed. Bob Dawson is widely hailed as the "father of juvenile justice" in Texas. It seems like a lofty status for a man who never worked in a juvenile court. Dawson is not from Tarrant County, although he would have been a welcome resident. Bob Dawson is a lawyer and served most of his legal career as a law professor at the University of Texas in Austin. His status comes from having written Title 3 of the family code, which is known simply as the Juvenile Justice code of Texas. "In his early years at UT, Dawson became known to his students as 'Mad Dog Dawson,' because he would push his students for better answers by leaning over his lectern and insisting 'Mad Dog wants more,' with a playful scowl."[214]

After initially writing the Juvenile Justice Code in Texas in 1973, in 1995 he became a part of a legislative power duo with Toby Goodman as they rewrote and expanded the Juvenile Justice Code. While the pendulum swung forcefully toward incarceration and a juvenile justice system that looked more like criminal justice, advocates believe that the 1995 code would have been incredibly draconian if not for the efforts of this pair of modern-day superheroes.[215]

"The code," Dawson said, according to the UT School of Law website, "recognized that kids could not be held fully responsible for their actions because they're not adults." Although it held them accountable with set sentences, it also provided that juveniles would be educated and trained for the best opportunity to straighten out their lives once they left the system.[216]

Toby Goodman got special permission for Dawson to be on the House floor during the 1995 debate on the bill. Together they worked to approve amendments that furthered Dawson's vision, and they defeated all but one amendment that didn't. Dawson credited Goodman with diverting "disaster," such as what occurred in other states where the age at which kids could be tried as adults was lowered as a way to address rising juvenile crime rates. "We did it," Dawson said, "without sacrificing any rights of kids, which I'm most proud of. It's so easy for juveniles to provoke adults to irrationality."[217]

As recounted on the UT school of law website, Robert Dawson shared how he stumbled into the role of architect of a state juvenile code:

I got the Texas teaching offer in 1968, and then two things happened that turned out to be very important to me, and Dean Page Keeton was really responsible for both of them. One was, the State Bar was in the process of revising the family law, the family code, making the family code, putting together all this stuff. Modernizing it. Texas family law was archaic at that time, particularly with regard to women's rights. It was just, you know, older and nineteenth century, as a matter of fact. In any event, they needed someone to do the juvenile justice portion of the family laws. . . . And Page knew that I had done work in juvenile justice, and so he said, "I can get money from the Hogg Foundation to give you a summer salary, if you want to work on that." So I said, "Yeah." So that summer of '68 I was working on my thesis, on my dissertation and I was . . . beginning to work on a juvenile justice code. And every other month I would go up to Dallas, and I had a committee of lawyers and I would present to them some sections that I had drafted over the past several weeks and we'd go over it and then we'd revise it and we just did that process. It took about four years. And we finally ended up with titles for the family code, which still exist in modified form. But that took from '68, we actually got the job done in '70, in '71, but the legislature rejected it; it was too liberal. But then with the Sharpstown scandal [a fraud scandal involving loans to state officials including the Texas Speaker of the House] and all the other stuff, we had that magic session of the legislature in 1973. The only session of the legislature that could probably be fairly characterized as liberal politically. And in that same session, they enacted the penal code and Titles two and three of the family code. So we got our law in place. So that was one development that occurred. I owe all of that to Page, because he didn't have to do that, I was the new kid on the block, but for whatever reason it was, he thought I could do the job and I have been active in juvenile justice ever since. I've been down at the legislature for virtually every session since 1973, and have written almost all of the juvenile laws in the state of Texas. I don't want to take credit for it. I write it, and committees go over it, and you know, the whole process. But I guess I would characterize myself as the principal draftsman of virtually all of the [juvenile] laws in the State of Texas and we've invented several things that have caught on nationally.[218]

Because of the work of Dawson, the state with the previously archaic law had become a model. In his words, "We have a juvenile justice system that quite honestly is regarded by most knowledgeable observers in the United States as one of the best available anywhere—which is remarkable for a state like Texas, which is not really known for social services."[219]

No one seems to dispute the leadership of of Goodman and Dawson during this time. While Goodman is still active outside of the legislature, Bob Dawson, after a fight with cancer, passed away in 2006. What is uncertain is who will fill the void that this combination has undoubtedly left in the legislative process. The work of these two men is carried on but is now on the shoulders of a multitude.

Riley Shaw

Riley Shaw is an assistant district attorney in Tarrant County, and until recently he served as the chief of the juvenile division in Tarrant County. He has practiced law for more than eighteen years and served with the Tarrant County District Attorney's office for much of his career. He is from Tarrant County and graduated from Nolan Catholic High School. He got his undergraduate degree at Texas Tech and then went on to finish law school at Tech as well. Shaw wanted to be a "real" trial attorney but initially found work as in-house counsel for homebuilder D.R. Horton. He eventually took a position at a civil litigation firm but never saw the inside of a courtroom.[220]

Riley met Mollee Westfall, now a judge in Tarrant County, on his first day as a 1L (first-year law student). By the time he was with the civil litigation firm, she was an assistant district attorney and remembered Riley sharing his dream of wanting to be a trial attorney. She called him in 2000 to inform him there was an opening for a prosecutor. Although he realized he would be taking about a 50 percent reduction in pay, Riley wanted to pursue the dream. He loved the work and enjoyed practicing law in the courtroom, where the rubber meets the road.[221]

Riley was sent to the juvenile section of the office in 2001. It would be an understatement to say that practicing juvenile law is seen by most prosecutors as a necessary evil on the path to being a felony prosecutor. For many it was at best a chance to learn something new; for others, it was a punishment. For a select few, it was a revelation of a new way of practicing law. Riley Shaw really enjoyed being assigned to the juvenile division. He was comfortable having an office north of downtown and at the department, and he saw the position as an opportunity. Shaw loved being in the courtroom, but like many involved in criminal justice, he had become frustrated with the idea of punishment as the only option to protect community safety. In a world where success was predicated on the number of years an offender was sentenced to serve, he found something new and even exciting in juvenile law. He had been exposed to the dream.[222]

Shaw understands that his role in prosecution is about protecting the community. Offenders should be accountable for their crimes and, if necessary, removed from the community to protect others. But in juvenile justice, he saw the reality that some young people have the potential to change, and public safety for the majority might actually mean that the juvenile should stay in the community and away from a correction system that tends to lead low-level offenders toward becoming higher risks to the community. He balanced this with the reality that some of the high-risk offenders, and those who committed the most serious offenses, needed removal from the community. Shaw's reality expanded to include the best interests of the young person as well as accountability to the public. After a little under a year in juvenile, Shaw was promoted to a position as a felony prosecutor and spent several years in different posts in various criminal courts. At one point he mentioned to one of the administrators then in the DA's office, David Montague, that he'd like to return to juvenile court should there ever be such an opportunity.[223]

Two years later, in 2004, that opportunity presented itself. Riley Shaw has worked in the juvenile division for the last twelve years and is one of very few prosecutors, and for that matter lawyers at large, who are board certified in juvenile law. His total length of service in the juvenile court is easily twice the length of service of those few prosecutors who have shown a particular interest in juvenile law in the county.[224]

In 2007, after the passing of Robert Dawson and the conclusion of service of Toby Goodman in the legislature, Riley Shaw attended a state-elected prosecutor meeting on behalf of Tarrant County before the 2007 state legislative session. The state's prosecutors were called together to address a need for a unified response to the issues surrounding abuse scandals at a West Texas (Pyote, Texas) Texas Youth Commission facility. In that case, a West Texas prosecutor had been sitting on evidence of abuse at the facility. The other prosecutors wanted to send the message that abuse, even if it involved young offenders in the state system, would not be tolerated.[225]

The prosecutors were given access to the Texas Juvenile Probation

Commission and TYC officials, in addition to the juveniles at the facilities, to see more closely what was happening at the state level in regard to the oversight of young people. Shaw's leadership skills became evident during the legislative process. In all, he ended up spending two and a half months in Austin giving a grounded perspective on concerns at the local level. He regularly contributes updates for *Texas Juvenile Law*, a book begun by Bob Dawson, considered the "lawnmower manual" of juvenile law in Texas. In 2013, Shaw was appointed by Governor Rick Perry to serve on Texas's violent gang task force. He was appointed to serve on the board of the Texas Juvenile Justice Department in 2015. Shaw has served as the treasurer and was the chair of the Juvenile Law Section of the State Bar of Texas for 2016. When there are questions about juvenile law, he has become one of the go-to persons throughout the state of Texas. Riley Shaw was offered a promotion to the Tarrant County District Attorney's administrative offices in 2017, ending his time as the chief of the juvenile division. As of 2018, Jim Hudson, another assistant district attorney who had a previous stint in the division, is serving as the division chief.

SEVEN

Continuity

What happens when the dreamer moves on or has a new dream? Too often, regardless of discipline in the ranks, something new takes root. Juvenile justice has often suffered from this circumstance, when someone new or some new research causes another shift in public opinion, causing the pendulum to swing again. Something "new" comes along, history repeats itself, and the dream is interrupted.

Another unique and embedded feature of the Tarrant County dream for juvenile justice is the continuity of leadership within the system and the ways that those involved in the system share institutional knowledge. There have been a number of ways this continuity has played out to the benefit of Tarrant County.

From the Bench

Judge Moore served in his role as a leader in the juvenile court for twenty-nine years in office and another several years in retirement. It is very difficult to find a political leader with that kind of staying power. The district attorney in Tarrant County during most of that term was one man, Tim Curry. What happens when a man or woman with that kind of presence or stability retires or moves on? Too often that absence creates a vacuum.

There is a saying that you can't have success without a successor. You could say that Judge Moore had a succession plan. He was a determined mentor and avoided the tendency of some leaders to hoard institutional knowledge as a way of holding on to power. In his wisdom, Judge Moore willingly passed on that knowledge and that power during his time in office. When he hired associate justices, he deliberately chose those who had experience in child welfare cases, who demonstrated a strong work ethic, and who shared his passion for protecting children. He felt that someone who could make wise and guarded decisions when a child's life hung in the balance would naturally do well in delinquency cases where decisions had a similarly serious impact on the lives of young people.

In 1987, when the Honorable Associate Judge Ernie Bates was appointed to another local bench, Moore made such a choice in Judge Jean Boyd. Judge Boyd served under his leadership for eight years before Moore's retirement. Boyd spoke of her initial frustration when Moore avoided complete answers to the questions of a young jurist. She would take questions to him, only to have him ask more questions. He would never give a complete answer but would help her clarify her own thinking about appropriate and lawful decisions in the cases she considered.[226]

Moore's mentoring bore full fruit upon his retirement in 1995, when Judge Boyd was elected as his replacement. She became only the second leader of the 323rd District Court, the Juvenile Court of Tarrant County. She has continued to use Moore's mentoring techniques with Judge Tim Menikos (who was also mentored by Judge Moore), Judge Ellen Smith (who worked as a family law attorney in Judge Moore's court), Judge Kimberly Brown, and Judge James Teel (who served as a prosecutor and a defense attorney in Judge Moore and Judge Boyd's court). They have each had the privilege of serving on the bench when Judge Moore was still active as a visiting retired district judge. Tarrant County also boasts the second largest number of certified juvenile law specialists, second only to Travis County, which includes a large percentage from their public defender's office—defense attorneys. Tarrant is unique in that each one of the juvenile court judges and the chief juvenile prosecutor all have their certifications.

Connections

The close interplay of personalities in Tarrant County juvenile work goes well beyond the bench. The most recent director of Juvenile Services was an assistant director under the previous director, Randy Turner. Mr. Medlin also served in Dallas County with Turner when he worked. Turner was mentored throughout his career by Carey Cockerell's two decades of leadership. In 1974, only months after Cockerell was back in Texas, Turner began his juvenile career as an intern at the very location where Cockerell was the assistant superintendent. In Turner's three decades of service, he worked under Cockerell in five different posts, including a year as the assistant director in

Tarrant County before taking over at Cockerell's retirement.[227]

State Representative Toby Goodman came in contact with the department during his tenure in office as the go-to person for any legislation dealing with system-involved youth. He and Bob Dawson began to learn about and rely upon the department as a resource during Goodman's time in office, further utilizing Tarrant County as a model for others to follow.[228]

Assistant District Attorney Riley Shaw began working with the legislature in 2007 as a young prosecutor with early exposure to the dream of juvenile justice. With the departure of Dawson and Goodman, the mantle of leadership in legislative circles and status as the go-to expert in juvenile law passed in part to Riley Shaw. Shaw also provided continuity within Tarrant County as the longest-serving juvenile prosecutor in the history of the division.

The State Orphans' Home of Corsicana was established in 1887 through the work of the Texas Woman's Christian Temperance Union, the group that established the Gatesville State Boys School in that same year to remove delinquent youth from the penitentiary system. In the 1930s, Lynn W. Ross and his wife were the directors of the boys' home of the orphanage. After this facility was transferred to the Texas Youth Commission, former directors Carey Cockerell and Randy Turner worked in the facility in the 1970s and 1980s, when it was called the Corsicana State Home. The reformers who began the dream in Texas were responsible for building the facility that employed three of the last four juvenile court directors. Sometimes destiny or providence is difficult to ignore.[229]

There have been several employees or connections in Tarrant County related to the teaching profession. One of the most respected in this arena was never an employee but has a not-so-distant connection to the department. Austin Porterfield was a professor at Texas Christian University for over three decades. He began his work in the field in 1937 and taught, even in retirement, up until his death in 1972. Porterfield wrote one of the earliest books on juvenile delinquency, *Youth in Trouble*. This book was published in 1946 with funds donated by a good friend, Leo Potishman.

Porterfield was the first in juvenile justice to publish a self-survey of delinquency, asking college students to report about contact with the juvenile authorities or things they had done that could have resulted in contact had they been discovered. His work continues to be mentioned for pioneering the idea of "hidden" delinquency, where those in college were involved in many of the same types of behaviors as those who entered the court system. The difference, he found, was in the level of support in the community for those who avoided arrest and labeling. He argued for the community to take on that supportive role for all young people. He also was unique in his belief that the parents were not the problem; like their children, they were simply products of the community at large and should be, along with the young person, a part of the solution.[230]

Dr. Porterfield's work in *Youth in Trouble* focused largely on the figures and practices of the work in Tarrant County. He recognized the need for the expansion of the dream. "The court is manned by earnest and sincere people, but it is understaffed, undertrained, overworked, and politically controlled. Moreover, the community does not know how near the court is built to the point where the human stream flows over the dam; and the community has affiliated with the court, but no child guidance clinic, no family service agency, no detention, no foster home care for delinquents."[231]

Dr. Porterfield influenced many Tarrant County students through his teaching. Not entirely coincidentally, perhaps, his grandson, the late Donald Willis, was married to Lyn Willis, the former assistant director for Tarrant County Juvenile Services and an employee for thirty-eight years. Jerry Wood, another assistant director and long-term employee, was a student at TCU who studied under some of Porterfield's colleagues in the sociology department.

Austin Porterfield, Paul Cromwell, Carey Cockerell, Jerry Wood, Vince Herdman, Jon Gustafson, Bill West, Christopher Bell, Angel Williams, and even Robert Dawson were known for teaching young minds who would serve in the field throughout the state of Texas and beyond. Henry Adams was quoted as saying, "A teacher affects eternity; he can never tell where his influence stops."[232] The influence these men have had is too far-reaching to put into words, but it makes the connections and the roots of Tarrant County Juvenile Services run deep.

The Culture
The other factor in continuity for the dream of juvenile justice belongs to the workers of the juvenile court, the probation staff. In part because of a boomer mentality, and in part due to the family atmosphere created and nurtured during the tenure of Lynn Ross, there is a remarkable career culture in the department. In interviewing many

of the staff, there is an amazing consistency in their stories. Many staff members either had never had exposure to juvenile justice or thought that they might use this to build experience that would lead them to other disciplines. But during their tenures the dream was planted, and passion for the work became a staple in their lives. There are several current employees who have worked for the last four directors. And there were two probation officers in Tarrant County who made the dream a reality for well over four decades of service: Sandra Williams and Don Dalton. Not only were they career employees, but they were remarkable employees whose examples shone for others.

A model organization doesn't endure on leadership and programming alone. It depends as well on the worker out front doing the everyday work of the court, the everyday work with young people and families, the one who creates and re-creates the dream of justice for juveniles. One sign of the strength of an organization's culture is when leaders emerge from within the organization. Many of those in the system have become leaders in just that way. Another sign of a vigorous culture is when leaders spread the seeds of the dream by taking root in other places.

There are so many people who have gone on to lead in other departments and in other facets of work with young people (school systems, advocacy groups, substance abuse clinics, mental health facilities, universities, publications, youth development work, and so on) that it would be impossible to mention and track them all. But it may be useful to list those workers who have served in Tarrant County Juvenile Services who have gone on to serve as directors in other counties. This is likely not an exhaustive list:

Mike Griffiths (Dallas County and TJJD), Charlie Skaggs (Williamson County), Mel Brown (Montgomery County), Jed Jutte (Palo Pinto County, Jack County), Mike Stack (Parker Adult), Sam Shanafelt (Wise County Adult), Bill Austin (Wise County), and Tom Kidd (Parker County).

EIGHT

If It Ain't Broke,
It's Still Worth Fixing

There is a movement across disciplines to focus less on deficits and more on strengths. This has been a difficult paradigm shift and probably more so in criminal justice systems than in most disciplines. In the past, the system was based on fixing what was broken. The movement toward bolstering *strengths* has a scientific basis. Unless a weakness or flaw is fundamental, many in this movement say that you should move the focus totally away from deficits. As a mindset, total blindness to deficits may be foolhardy, however. Some of the high points in the history of Tarrant County Juvenile Services may be those times the department addressed some of its darker moments. It is a matter of balance.

The story of any person or organization would be incomplete if the less-than-flattering moments were left out. The character of a person or institution isn't determined by bad choices and decisions; it's developed when those involved choose to learn from those experiences and move forward in the aftermath—emphasizing the positive, and learning from the negative. This chapter will look at the latter, those moments that might have derailed the dream if the dreamers hadn't the constant discipline to reexamine the process moving toward it.

Missing Ingredient

Any cook will tell you that if you miss a key ingredient, you might be in trouble. Even the best of cooks may not be able to compensate for what isn't there. Despite being an early leader in so many initiatives, the Tarrant County Juvenile Court was strapped for almost seventy years without a key ingredient—a juvenile detention center that was separate and apart from the adult jail.

There were several dreamers within Tarrant County Juvenile Services who took up this cause unsuccessfully. In 1913, Sam Callaway called for a detention home and publicly talked about the urgency of the need during his tenure. Two close friends even got into a public debate about the topic. In May of 1947, Leo Potishman and Austin Porterfield traded op-ed pieces in the *Fort Worth Star-Telegram*. Potishman, a lifelong children's advocate despite having none of his own, indicated that a detention home would require entirely too much money for such a small population. Dr. Porterfield enjoyed Mr. Potishman's company but not always his ideology. In a rebuttal, Dr. Porterfield pointed out that there needed to be a center not only for the small portion who would be detained, but as a proper place for the thousands of kids each year (1,048 in 1946) who were picked up by law enforcement but never stayed in the county jail. "The chief need is not merely for a detention home, but for a child study center with trained workers. This center should be open for referrals by the police of all arrests of children, seven days a week, twenty-four hours a day."[233]

While the importance of a detention center was argued for decades, no one had the resolve or the tenacity to bring one into being until Lynn Ross. From the beginning of Ross's tenure, he realized the need for an institution that was separate and apart from the adult system—a basic tenet of juvenile justice. For the span of his career he determinedly pursued such an institution.

In 1955, the Tarrant County Crime Commission put together an interesting trip, with a lunch and a police escort, for county leaders who were involved in working with juveniles. Lynn Ross, the county sheriff, and other leaders toured the existing Tarrant County facilities and then made their way to Dallas to visit their neighbor's facilities. All who participated agreed that Dallas had superior facilities in every way. The Tarrant County Crime Commission chairman, Clyde Weed, revealed that the commission knew there was a sharp contrast; he got the Tarrant County leaders together in the hope of kicking off a campaign to create a similar facility in Tarrant County. Weed noted that more than once in the previous thirty years, bond programs for juvenile institutions had failed, but that was when only one or two organizations were supporting it. This had been a thorn in the side of Tarrant County leaders for thirty years. "This time, we've gained the support of practically every civic organization in the county. Each one of us on today's tour [thirty-five individuals] will go back to his organization and report what we saw," Weed said.[234]

In 1965, Judge Moore joined the impassioned cry for a new center. In fact, this had been a focus from the beginning of Tarrant County's juvenile court with Judge Terrell. Lynn Ross and Judge Moore beat the drum persistently, with measure, and largely without result, despite their presence and reputation.[235]

In 1966, a *Dallas Morning News* article quoted Ross as saying that Tarrant County was behind the curve. "We're one of the few major counties which still keep juveniles in the county jail," he said. "It's probably true that a short stay in jail may help some juveniles by serving as a shock treatment and letting them know what they face if they don't change their ways," Ross said. "But for every boy it helps, a dozen more are hurt." Lynn Ross also wanted to make it clear to administrators that a new lockup would not be sufficient. He said a staff would need to be present to watch over the young people, monitoring attitudes and behavior and providing counseling as well as educational and recreational activities. "Unless commissioners are willing to provide this staff, I would rather not have a detention home. We don't need another place to lock juveniles up." The only report of a response, from the county auditor, was his concern that taxpayers would object to such an idea.[236]

A Measure of Success

In 1957, county leaders won a small victory when a center for predelinquent youth (truants and runaways) was built near Eagle Mountain Lake, a bit northwest of Fort Worth in Tarrant County.[237] It wasn't a detention center, but it would help keep some kids from going into the state school system.

It was a partnership between the City of Fort Worth and the private sector. Fort Worth leased a twenty-five-acre parcel of land to the county at the cost of one dollar a year, while the Fort Worth Council of Jewish Women and the Junior League of Fort Worth put up most of the money for construction of the building on the site. The cost was approximately $90,000 for what was initially a six-thousand-square-foot facility. It was simply known as the Tarrant County Youth Center until it was renamed in the 1970s for a judge and previous juvenile board member, Judge Joe Eidson.[238]

In 2002, a financial decision was largely responsible for the permanent closure of the Eidson Youth Center. Without fanfare or much fuss, except maybe from the workers who had invested their careers, the center was shuttered. The cost of making a building constructed half a century earlier accessible to the handicapped seemed prohibitive; a cost-benefit analysis concluded that dollars could better be used to enhance community-based services.

HEW

In 1967, when Judge Moore was serving as the sole jurist of the first designated court for juveniles, the department asked the federal government to provide an outside, unbiased, expert perspective on its operations. Workers from the federal Department of Health, Education, and Welfare (HEW) were invited to conduct an investigation of the entire department. This required an unusual perspective from leadership.[239]

How often do we openly invite the perspective of others? Even among close friends, it takes a special kind of relationship to invite possible criticism. It is often needed, and healthy, but humbling at the same time.

What if you have been seen as a model for others to follow? What happens if the results aren't favorable? Do you take the chance to voluntarily have a government authority expose your weaknesses to you and others? The HEW inspection was a risk, but Judge Moore had an agenda.

The HEW report, after investigation and monitoring conducted by a four-man team, was highly critical of the department. It called for a "total new look" in caring for juveniles. It said Tarrant County had fallen down on the job in serving juveniles, and that the "penny-pinching" ways of the Commissioner's Court was to blame. HEW recommended a juvenile detention center with at least thirty beds, a full-time juvenile court, the removal of responsibility for dependency and neglect cases by transferring those cases to the state department of public welfare, and the removal of other nonprobation duties from a staff stretched too thin. The report urged higher salaries to attract and keep qualified staff, higher pay for foster parents, and the appointment of a citizen's committee whose role was to keep the public informed about the work of the county.

The four-man team of investigators further said the county should only be detaining about 2 percent of the roughly fifteen hundred juveniles who had been detained in the county jail over the past year. They indicated the department should have a full-time probation officer on duty. At the time, officers left at 4:30 p.m., and police who made arrests after that were left to make detention decisions. Probation officers often released detainees the next working day without a hearing. The investigators felt this was possibly infringing on the youths' constitutional rights to a hearing.[240]

Upon receiving the report, Judge Moore quickly requested that the juvenile board have a full-time juvenile court and also take steps toward the building of a detention center. Many of the other reforms recommended were quickly put into place: night screening by a probation officer, juvenile workers at the jails to work proactively with the kids under their supervision, and fewer kids in jail.[241]

The report had successfully turned up the heat on county authorities. There was now real pressure to provide a new center. Architects were hired, visits to other successful centers throughout the country were made, and sites were pondered. Despite the pressure, it was a painfully slow process—too slow.

It Took a Tragedy

Too often, a change everyone knows needs to happen happens too late. The creation of a juvenile detention center in Tarrant County was unfortunately one of those instances. The dream of juvenile justice is to protect kids from making decisions that will hurt them, to protect those that need protecting. As difficult as it is to admit, even from the beginning, the dream has failed young people. There are probably many instances of this in Tarrant County, as there are way too many in the system at large, but on an evening in January 1969, Tarrant County failed in an irreversible and tragic way.

Grady was a young man in need of protecting, a young man whose path had brought him into contact with the juvenile justice system— often a traumatic experience for children and their families. Nationally, less than 5 percent of young people cross paths with the juvenile justice system, but when it does happen, despite the path or circumstances, families struggle to come to grips with all that it entails. The juvenile court was designed to bring about rehabilitation, so that the young people who move through it will come out on the other side having learned and grown from the experience. The system is now better prepared to equip young people and families. Grady, however, didn't get the opportunity to experience a better system.

Before there was a juvenile detention center, young people who were kept in the juvenile ward of the county jail were placed in a separate wing, apart from adults. Police matrons were present to occasionally check in on the residents. Most juvenile-specific detention centers are designed as short-term responses to illegal or unhealthy behavior. Those centers that serve as preadjudication facilities (before any delinquency judgment or punishment—in adult terms, before conviction) are designed to be places for stabilization, where young people stay briefly until court or other arrangements can be made.

Grady had been a resident at the county youth center, a nonsecure residential placement for young people who were not making very good decisions in their home environments. On Thursday, January 1, 1968, Grady became quite upset and began to act out at the center. For these reasons, he was taken to the juvenile ward of the county jail. The staff prepared a transition on Thursday with a plan for Grady to return to the center on Friday morning. In a transition designed to help young men like Grady stabilize without disrupting the program at the center, Grady was placed in a cell with other youths on Thursday evening. He became combative, however, and was moved to a private cell. Within thirty minutes of being isolated, he fashioned his shirt into a noose and hung himself. All of the many reasons for a new center now had a tragic face.[242]

Political Will

Two men of great presence and reputation—Lynn Ross and Scott Moore—had joined forces to push forward reforms. There was a countywide recognition of a need since a federal agency, HEW, had blasted the department and its facilities. And there had been the tragic loss of a young life. If years of pressure and these recent events could not move the county to act, what would be required? Political will.

The impediment to changing the status quo was that the population involved children. If resources are going to be spent on children, where do we start? Typically, it is with children who are doing well, or on resources that would help them continue to do well, such as schools. The labels we apply matter, and let's face it, involvement with juvenile delinquents does not make political careers—unless being "tough on (juvenile) crime" is the byword.

Constituents matter to politicians, and constituents do not want adult or juvenile offenders in their backyards. With so much bad news coming our way, it is hard to blame the public for such feelings, but sins of omission can still do much harm. Mounting evidence shows that continuing to keep juveniles with adults, or in prison-like settings, is at best an ineffective tool for rehabilitation; at worst, it can be fatal to an individual's prospects when that individual becomes your neighbor again.

Even if officials could find a "backyard" that wasn't near a neighborhood, there was the issue of money. The same people who don't want such centers in their backyards also don't want to pay for them to be in someone else's. The politician has a difficult time selling taxpayers on expending resources for juvenile delinquents when that money could perhaps smooth out the potholes in their roads.

To take up this cause was risky. It might turn public opinion against you. People willing to put others above themselves would need to be involved. Lynn Ross and Scott Moore were the perfect match for such a cause. They didn't mind making the hard decisions, and it was about the dream, not about them. This is a pretty rare quality to find in people, and rarer still in politics or in the bureaucracy. Longtime Fort Worth mayor Mike Moncrief described it this way: "Have you ever seen a frozen pond? Have you ever seen a sign on that pond that said, 'Danger, Thin Ice!'? Have you ever wondered who put it there? That is Scott Moore. He was willing to take risks and put himself in harm's way for what is right." What happens when you combine two such men on the same project with the same goal?

Not in My Backyard: The Poor Farm

Although the tragic loss of Grady's life coming on the heels of the damning report from HEW should have doubled the pace at which changes were made, it took the game of baseball and another two full years for change to come about.

Over the next two years, discussion about where the money would come from and where the site would be located dominated meetings of the juvenile board and the Commissioner's Court. A total of four sites were considered. Initially the old LaGrave Field, just north of downtown, was considered after the semipro baseball team temporarily ceased playing there. Two other sites received a lot of attention, both in Southeast Tarrant County. One was 4700 South Riverside Drive, formerly the Crippled Children and Adult Rehabilitation Center—property already owned by the county. There were concerns about renovating this existing property, however, to meet the needs of the detention center. [243] Another site that won temporary approval from the commissioners lay along Sycamore Creek Road, east of Lancaster and west of Beach Street, but the group was still debating whether or not a center costing an estimated $3 million should be built at all.[244]

Final agreement on the site was not without controversy. The one chosen was the old poor farm in Fort Worth, which, up until the early 1960s, served another vulnerable population. It housed the poor and the elderly and also housed a tuberculosis (TB) sanatorium. Many of the former residents were buried onsite, and their remains had to be reinterred in nearby cemeteries.

The Texas State Historical Association provides some of the history on what constituted a poor farm in Texas:

> Poor farms are defined by the *American Heritage Dictionary* as "A farm that houses, supports, and employs the poor at the public's expense." Poor farms were the predecessor to modern-day welfare and served as society's dumping grounds for outcasts. Those who were insane, tubercular, deaf, imbecile, criminal, aged, or poor were often placed together on county poor farms. The inmates were viewed as hopeless and useless. Prior to the Great Depression, America's poor were handled within a system that evolved from seventeenth-century English poor laws, and generally provided minimal relief and involved limited government services. American colonists transplanted Elizabethan England methods of care for the poor, emphasizing poverty as disgraceful and providing relief strictly to avoid disorder, not out of charitable ideals.[245]

Texas poor farms had little, if any, interaction with the public. The poor farm system was created in an attempt to deal with a problem, but the system was not afforded the resources of other government entities. The residents held insignificant community standing. "The first mention of a county poor farm in Texas can be found within the 1869 constitution. Article XII, section 26 reads, 'Each county in the State shall provide, in such a manner as may be prescribed by law, a Manual Labor Poor House, for taking care of, managing, employing, and supplying the wants of its indigent and poor inhabitants; and under such regulations as the legislature may direct, all persons committing petty offenses in the county may be committed to such Manual Labor Poor House for correction and employment.'"[246]

As a result of the provision Texas required county governments to take responsibility for their poor. "The provision reinforced two popular nationwide beliefs: 1) Care was to be based on the principle of 'less eligibility' (that the conditions on the poor farm would be worse than conditions outside to deter dependence) and 2) assistance was never intended to provide a life as comfortable as that which non-recipients had."[247]

In the Lone Star State, Texans who survived the frontier experience viewed rugged individualism as a value and gave applause to opportunity and success. Dependence on others is not seen as a respectable trait. Texas required poor farm residents to take an oath swearing "to their lack of goods and their desperate need for assistance."[248] Residents were required to forfeit any semblance of control of their personal lives and their basic rights as citizens—including their right to vote—and moved to the poor farm. These practices served to deter anyone considering life on the poor farm. Desperation and forfeiture of pride would likely mark those who sought shelter in the poor farm.

The rise of other federal relief programs served to render poor farms unnecessary. The Texas State Historical Association recalled this somewhat forgotten history. "The Texas poor farm has become a mythical part of our past, even though poor houses and farms have been around for hundreds of years, and some were operating into the 1960s. Little is known today of the state's early attempts at government intervention during times of individual and national crisis, and even some of the most seasoned Texans do not recall their county's poor farm or even realize that 'the poor farm' was anything other than an expression."[249]

So after decades of neglecting poor farm residents, the county had decided to give the site to another neglected population—juvenile offenders. History, it seems, does have a way of repeating itself. This was a backyard that had few neighbors other than industrial businesses and a cemetery. It was property owned by the county. Finally, a place the politicians could agree on. There was only one more bridge to cross: money for building the facility.

At the time of the agreement, $850,000 was set aside for construction.[250] It would not be enough. Eventually, the county sold some land it owned, the Arlington Turnpike, a parcel that would later become the home for minor league baseball and the team that would become the Texas Rangers. It was money from this sale that finally provided the needed funding to build the center, which was completed in March 1971.[251]

After almost eighty years of waiting, the detention center built in 1971 was considered a state-of-the-art-facility. Two wings were initially constructed: a fifteen-bed boys' wing (the A wing) and an eleven-bed girls' wing (the B wing). There was a woodworking shop, a cosmetology center, a gymnasium, and a workout room.[252]

The Features of the Early Center

Though it was a long time in the making, the center was a first-rate facility. The design for the detention center was created after the planners looked at five centers across the country. The individual cells, cinder blocks instead of bars, and even the paint for the center were intentionally chosen. As additions were made, other distinctive features were brought forward, such as natural light and courtyards to allow inmates some access to open sky.

The staff was also carefully chosen. Lynn Ross believed that the same requirements should be in place for the workers in detention as there were for probation officers and required that workers in the center have college degrees.

The center has been expanded several times to house bigger populations and eventually to include the entire operations of the juvenile department. The complex now carries the names of the two leaders most responsible for its existence: The Scott D. Moore Juvenile Justice Center and the Lynn W. Ross Detention Center. In 1977, the expansion included a courtroom for the 323rd District Court—the juvenile court—and offices for the probation staff. In 1991, two additional wings with thirty new detention beds were added, along with additional office space. In 1999, a major renovation of the center was completed. This allowed for yet another courtroom, a modernization and remodeling to include a new entrance, four pods with seventy-two new beds, new classrooms, additional office space for a growing staff, and a training facility. There are plans for yet another expansion expected by 2020.

The leadership in the center over the years has been overseen by the following individuals: Tom Foster, Neil Jones, Mel Brown, Randall Hatley, Chuck Pearce, Charlie Skaggs, Gerald Ray, Peggy Tucker, Hope Harris, Ron Lewis, and Jesus Reyes.

The Dirty Seven and Paul Cromwell

The departure of Paul Cromwell is not one of the particularly bright moments in the history of the department. He resigned because, in his words, he had become "too unpopular to be an effective leader." People speak in hushed tones about the circumstances that led to his departure. Most employees who were around the department at that time still say, "If you want to know about that, you can find it in the newspapers." A quarter of a century later they are still wary. Few institutions make it into the papers because things are going well. Tarrant County Juvenile Services appears in the paper when young people commit very adult crimes or very adolescent ones. It also makes it into the paper when officers make stupid decisions and, too often, when there is an abuse of a child's trust.

The department in the early 80s included a group known as the Dirty Seven. The seven represented a majority of the supervisors in the department (out of nine total) who expressed displeasure in the leadership of Paul Cromwell. Their confidence in their leader began to unravel slowly, an unraveling that accelerated when he confronted their dissatisfaction by revealing a stack of applications for their positions. Walking into the room of supervisors with a pipe in his mouth, he declared, "I hear some people don't like it here. I have a bunch of people who would like to be in your position."[253]

Over the last several years of Cromwell's tenure, the Dirty Seven began to document instances of his abuse of authority, utilizing what might look like espionage—after-hours investigations, illuminated by flashlights. Four years before it would come to a head, members of the juvenile board asked the FBI to investigate potential misappropriation of federal dollars.[254] Eventually, with the aid of attorney Allan Butcher, who was also a professor at the University of Texas at Arlington, the supervisors went to the juvenile board with two complaints of abuse of power: 1) misuse of county-sponsored Explorer Scout funds for personal use and 2) circumvention of standard and legal hiring practices by hiring some of his (Cromwell's) students at Texas Christian University without following the standard human resource process. Paul Cromwell resigned, and the Dirty Seven were still unsatisfied. They wanted an investigation.

The juvenile board organized a small investigative team. The findings of this team were dissected by the entire board for a week, and they concluded they could find no evidence that would have even resulted in discipline, much less termination. By this time, the story made the local paper, and Cromwell bade farewell to government life, pursuing his education instead. Since the Dirty Seven, Paul Cromwell, and others remain largely silent about the event, it isn't clear if there were other unresolved issues or just unreliable memories of the issues, and it isn't entirely clear whether the board, despite its findings, did the merely expedient thing by accepting the resignation and moving on.[255]

It wasn't without cost to those who stood up for the integrity of the department and the children of Tarrant County. Four of the Dirty Seven, after they had put themselves on the line in Tarrant County, went on to continue work in other parts of Texas. Possibly coincidentally, the county began drafting a code of conduct, published in 1984, that set out minimum ethical expectations for its employees.[256]

As it is in any organization, clarity comes from learning when to take a stand and publicly expose organizational problems and when to close ranks and deal with conflict within the organization without involving outside attention and damaging the reputation of the organization itself. There is a fine line here, and crossing it can have an adverse impact on an organization's culture. Cromwell ultimately put the health of the organization above his own interests. In this business of juvenile justice, egos, agendas, and politics are inevitable, but if the dream is to be realized, these have to yield to the primary goal of helping young people find their way.

Separate but Equal?

The state of Texas has come a long way in race relations but has much further to go. In September 1948, Lynn Ross hired a caseworker in child support services with a master's degree and some history in the world of education. In the late 1940s, it seems those kinds of credentials would hold value. But what if the person was a woman? Furthermore, what if the woman was not white?

When Eula Hortense Chatman entered the organization, the United States had not yet undergone the civil rights struggle of the 1960s. It was the height of the Jim Crow era, dominated by laws that created "separate but equal" public places throughout the United States. It was also prior to the Supreme Court ruling in *Brown v. Board of Education* that ended segregation in schools and well prior to the Civil Rights Act of 1964, which put an end to the notion of separate being equal.

In that world, Chatman went to work for Tarrant County Juvenile Services. She was the first African American professional employed by any department in the county. Despite her remarkable qualifications, this fact would have implications for Ross, the department, and most importantly, for Chatman.

She was not allowed to work alongside her colleagues at the Tarrant County courthouse. Instead, arrangements for her office space were made with the Baker Funeral Home, a historic African American funeral home in Fort Worth, approximately three miles south of the courthouse. The county paid the funeral home $25 per month rent for her office. At the time, Chatman supervised a caseload of primarily African American females. Even in the early sixties, after the civil rights movement began and Chatman was allowed to have an office with her colleagues, she was asked to use a separate entrance. Inexcusable as such treatment was, it's apparent that Lynn Ross pushed the envelope when he hired Eula Chatman.[257]

Robert Woodert, hired in 1966, indicated he could only work with an all-African American caseload.[258] Ross's efforts led to the hires in the 1960s of Dolores Hogans, Robert Woodert, and other African Americans, but the county was slow to address another critical need: Hispanic officers. It wasn't until some twenty years after the hiring of Eula Chatman that Tarrant County Juvenile Services hired the first Hispanic officer, Alfred Briones, in 1969.[259] And it wasn't until the early 1990s that the first female Hispanic officer, Belinda Hampton, was hired.

Sixty years later, the department and the county still struggle to ensure equal treatment for both workers and clients. Over the last five years, the department has been involved in an ongoing effort with the Mental Health Connection, an advocacy group, to move toward a system that is equipped to address these cultural competency issues. In August 2016, the department hired its first African American director. There is still a long way to go. In many ways, the movement toward equal treatment for everyone associated with Tarrant County Juvenile Services began with the courage of Eula Hortense Chatman.

NINE

A Difference Maker

Judge John Terrell was the first judge to serve in Tarrant County's juvenile court and was a national advocate in the early days of the dream. Judge Jean Boyd is a dedicated professional with a passion for helping young people who has continued and added to the dream. Judge Timothy Menikos carries the torch now. Whether in historical archives or in interviews with those who have done the work, the focus almost always comes back to the judge.

Although it is easy to recognize the influence of each jurist who has ascended to the bench over the years, Judge Scott Moore, possibly more than any other individual, had a singular and enduring impact on the dream of juvenile justice for Tarrant County and beyond. It is hard to read the words of one of the United States' first juvenile court judges, Judge Julian Mack, without thinking of this man. "The child who must be brought into court should, of course, be made to know that he is face to face with the power of the state," Mack stated in 1909, "but he should at the same time, and more emphatically, be made to feel that he is the object of its care and solicitude."[260]

Such an equilibrium was present throughout the tenure of Scott Moore. Judge Moore, who gave three decades of his life furthering the dream of juvenile justice, embodied the perfect blend of the authority of the state and the care, solicitude, and empathy of a father figure. He often held court, or at least portions of it, without his formal robe, in his chambers, and seated next to the young man or woman in question with the attorney, probation officer, and at times parents present. He lost none of his dignity, while benefitting the child, the court, and the county immensely.

Judge Scott Moore never required the staff of the juvenile court to do anything he would not do, but he set the bar high. All he asked of himself was to give everything he had for the best interest of the youth he served. Moore also knew intuitively that detention was a last resort and contributed what might possibly be one of the fastest dockets in the nation so that children would receive the appropriate care and treatment as quickly as possible.

Scott Moore partnered with juvenile justice authorities and providers whether they wanted him to or not, and most often, they did. Judge Moore made things happen when others couldn't. Mike Moncrief said it this way: "There was no quit in the man." If he took up a cause, it would be won. Judge Moore held every individual accountable for the work performed to help a child. And he expected the work to be done deliberately, without haste. He held tightly to the dream and made sure anyone who had an impact on the system held tightly as well. He was a rare man who could hold true to a vision that was a century old yet employ evidence-based procedures before the concept was even conceived. He was gentle yet stern. He was at times southern and country, yet he remained refined and dignified. He was the man—the judge.[261]

TEN

Conclusion: A Model for the Pursuit of the Dream?

The 2011 session of the Texas state legislature, as a major source of focus, abolished the two state juvenile justice agencies in order to overhaul a system that in many ways was considered broken, if not destroyed. While many felt that reforms that began in 2009 were still in process, the institutional side of juvenile probation continued to be investigated for instances of abuse. This decision has also had an impact on the community side of juvenile justice in the state.

When one agency seems broken, and the other seems to be functioning as intended, what is the purpose of abolishing both? It brings to mind the old expression of throwing out the baby with the bathwater. One has to wonder if the same would have occurred if the institutional side of the system had been operating smoothly.

An additional part of the reform in the 2011 legislative session was to close three facilities; two others had been closed in the preceding years. Research that has supported keeping kids closer to their homes supports the strategy of jettisoning old, rural institutions. Closing institutions is potentially a step in the right direction for our state, but only if Texas is serious about taking a step back to look at the original dream for juvenile justice.

In place of these two agencies, a new agency has now emerged: the Texas Juvenile Justice Department. The concern is that this is more about fiscal responsibility than it is about helping young people. The hope is that restructuring is the first step toward meaningful reform to help change lives.

As it existed in the past, not only did the Texas system often fail to prevent delinquency, it too often actually endangered the children in its care. Young people in the system very rarely got the sort of care, education, or programs that have been shown to keep them from offending again after release. Although reforms occurred over and over again, bringing some progress, the system as a whole has never fully realized the dream, and has at times nearly destroyed it.

Although this latest overhaul has improved the system, more work is needed. Retooling provides an opportunity for meaningful reform, but it does not guarantee it. There is promising language in the legislation, but the success of these changes hinges on how the law is implemented, who is doing the implementing, and who is watching to see that reforms are done right and are sustained over time. Young people will require bold, strong leaders experienced in best practices to take the reins immediately and for the long term. There have to be diligent guardians of the dream.

It only takes a perusal of the headlines across the United States to see that some will even blame a community-focused approach on any problems that come forward from closing facilities. Recent headlines revealed that when a seventeen-year-old in state detention at Tryon Girls Center in Fulton County, New York, was told that "she had to wait to make a phone call, state police said she stabbed a male staffer in the face with a pencil. It was part of what law enforcement officials describe as escalating teen violence against staff even as New York continues closing juvenile prisons and sending more troubled youths to community-based programs."[262] At Tryon, workers faulted the permissive policies of Commissioner Gladys Carrión, an advocate of alternatives to youth prisons since she became head of New York's Office of Children and Family Services. Carrión says research consistently shows better outcomes when young offenders are closer to home and not sent to distant, costly detention centers, and she recently proposed closing four more. The list includes Tryon Girls Center; the adjacent boy's detention center in Johnstown closed last year.[263]

The prosecutor and investigator who review reported incidents at Tryon say they have seen more violence by juveniles against staff since facilities began closing. "The facility has been in anarchy," said Fulton County District Attorney Louise K. Sira. "I think it's related to the policy at the state level."[264]

Clearly, when someone within a system initiates reform, it is tough. Resistance within the system was demonstrated by state school guards in Texas when the early TYC attempted to institute reforms. But when movements toward reform come from one segment of a combined system where community-based practices and institutions are roommates in the same building, as they are in New York and now Texas, evidence from one may be seen as a threat to the existence of the other. Carrión has made some curious decisions, but her opponents claim that every negative event within the system is directly or indirectly related to the push for reform. Few speak of all the negative events that occurred before the reform efforts. Logic and rational thought are often overwhelmed by emotion. Evidence to the contrary, building or securing additional facilities is viewed as a sure—read quick—solution to the problem of juvenile crime.

If children must be removed from the community for a time, their successful rehabilitation requires caring for and providing useful services during their stay. Caretakers must provide meaningful reentry services and serve juveniles close to home, in the community or in small facilities, when necessary. Families must be involved in the rehabilitation process, and kids must have opportunities to remain connected with the community when appropriate. The core concept of juvenile justice is that young offenders have the capacity to change. Taking that idea seriously seems to be a tall order for a system that heard precisely these sentiments from Richard Clendenen in 1948 and from so many others before and since.

Local and state officials must work in partnership and hold one another accountable for what happens to kids after they enter the system. Communities must make sure that the children from and in their communities are safe. This is going to require making juvenile justice a shared responsibility, with no voice being more important than another.

It will take renewed vigilance to have a juvenile justice department that works. Otherwise, we risk putting a new face on an old way of doing business that does little to redirect children in trouble or to improve public safety in the long run.

The danger in any system is to think it has arrived. In the book *Good to Great*, Jim Collins looked at what makes the difference between those companies that sustained growth and those that plateaued, and suggested some simple reasons for the difference. Collins said, "More than anything else, real people, in real companies, want to be a part of a winning team. They want to contribute to producing real results. They want to feel the excitement and the satisfaction of being part of something that just flat-out works. When people begin to feel the magic of momentum—when they begin to see tangible results and can feel the flywheel start to build speed—that's when they line up, throw their shoulders to the wheel, and push." Tarrant County saw these results and experienced that excitement and satisfaction early. As Collins said, "Great vision with mediocre people still produces mediocre results." It takes the vision and the people.[265]

As any organization must, Tarrant County's juvenile court has made adjustments to the political winds buffeting it, but its policies include bedrock elements that have kept the mission on track. Those elements are an evidence-based approach, community-based services, a commitment to engage the family as an integral part of the child's rehabilitation, partnerships with community organizations and services outside of the system, brief interactions with institutions when necessary, excellence in service delivery, and a focus on building strengths in youth and their families. These elements—some of them new ideas, some of them not so new—are nationally recognized as essential to practices that result in positive development for troubled kids.

Tarrant County Juvenile Services has had moments when the dream seems stifled, but the dream is as resilient as it is contagious. The juvenile department at Tarrant County came close to collapse in 1910 and almost again in the late 1960s. In an act of courage, the department, under Judge Scott Moore, invited HEW to assess its services. The report was scathing and might have crushed lesser men and women. Instead, it fanned the flames of reform among those inside the system, thanks to the leadership, vision, and passion of the dreamers. You can still feel the sting of that event when you talk to those who were there. It was more than uncomfortable. Knowing and claiming the dream of juvenile justice made HEW's findings totally unconscionable.

A dream that doesn't last usually dies from the inside. The person or organization changes, or perhaps those involved never firmly grasped the essential nature of the dream in the first place. This is where leadership matters—never resting after achieving a goal, but always looking toward the next goal, and then the next.

In *Burning Down the House*, author Nell Bernstein concluded that young people most needed two things: support and connection.[265] For decades, Tarrant County Juvenile Services has recognized these fundamentals, remaining focused on turning young people's lives around. That focus must be the central theme of turning around the troubled history of our state's juvenile justice system. With the implementation of the 2011 legislation, it is clear that a new chapter has opened for juvenile justice in Texas. If the dream is to continue, we will all be responsible for writing what happens next.

Notes by Chapter

Introduction
1. *Inception*, directed and written by Christopher Nolan (Warner Brothers, 2010).
2. Julian W. Mack, "The Juvenile Court," *Harvard Law Review*, no. 23 (1909): 120.
3. "The Boy and the Law," *El Paso Herald*, February 5, 1910.
4. Mack, "The Juvenile Court," 120.
5. Robert E. Sullivan, *Macaulay: The Tragedy of Power* (Cambridge, MA: Harvard University Press, 2009), 397.
6. "Juvenile Court Plans: Judge Terrell Claims County Has First Court," *Dallas Morning News*, December 5, 1910.

Chapter 1
7. John Augustus, *A Report on the Labors of John Augustus for the Last Ten Years: In Aid of the Unfortunate* (Boston: Wright & Hasty Printers, 1852), 34.
8. Joan Petersilia, "Probation in the United States: Part 1," *Crime and Justice* 22, (1997): 33.
9. Hans Peter Mareus Neilsen, ed., *The Laws of Texas* (Austin: Gammel Book Company, 1907), 13:137-140.
10. Neilsen, *The Laws of Texas*, 137-140.
11. Pauline Periwinkle, "Save the children: Texas legislators to be asked to establish juvenile courts in the state; Industrial school adjunct—Gatesville reformatory may be converted into a manual training school for idle boys," *Dallas Morning News*, January 10, 1904.
12. Kevin Maillard, "Rethinking Children as Property," *Surface 75* (Summer 2012), http://surface.syr.edu/lawpub/75.
13. Sarah Steward-Lindsey, "Fulfilling the Promise of Kent: Fixing the Texas Juvenile Waiver Statute," *American Journal of Criminal Law* 34, no. 1 (2006): 109.
14. "The History of Juvenile Justice," *American Bar Association Division for Public Education*, 4; Kristen Orlando, People v. Nguyen: A Modern Look at the Use of Juvenile Adjudications as Strike Offenses Under the Three Strikes Law, *Santa Clara Law Review* 55 (2015): 917, http://www.americanbar.org/content/dam/aba/migrated/publiced/features/DYJpart1.authcheckdam.pdf
15. In re Gault, 387 US 1 (1967).
16. In re Gault.
17. In re Gault.
18. "Part 1. The history of juvenile justice." ABA Division for Public Education, http://www.americanbar.org/content/dam/aba/migrated/publiced/features/DYJpart1.authcheckdam.pdf.
19. In re Winship, 397 US 358 (1970).
20. In re Winship.
21. In re Winship.
22. "A Brief History of the Texas Juvenile Justice Department," (April 2016), www.lbb.state.tx.us/Documents/Publications/issue_Briefs/3082_Brief_History_TX_JJD.pdf.
23. Morales v. Turman, 326 F. Supp. 677 (E.D. Tex. 1971).
24. "A Brief History of the Texas Juvenile Justice System," http://www.lbb.state.tx.us/Documents/Publications/Issue_Briefs/3082_Brief_History_TX_JJD.pdf.

25. Ruby Shaw and Everette B. Penn, Texas State Supplement to Chapter 5 of Cox, S. M. et al. (2011). *Juvenile Justice: A Guide to Theory, Policy, and Practice*, http://www.sagepub.com/juvenilejustice7e/study/state/texas/TexasJuvenileJusticeSup-pch05.pdf.
26. "A Brief History of the Texas Juvenile Justice System."
27.Shaw and Penn, Texas State Supplement to Chapter 5 of Cox, S. M. et al., *Juvenile Justice: A Guide to Theory, Policy, and Practice*.
28. Jennifer Warren, *One in 100: Behind Bars in America 2008* (Pew Center on the States, February 2008).
29. Bureau of Justice Statistics, *Correctional Populations in the United States, 2016* (April 2018), https://www.bjs.gov/content/pub/pdf/cpus16.pdf.
30. *The Greatest Reform School in the World: A Guide to the Records of the New York House of Refuge* (New York State Archives, 1989), http://www.archives.nysed.gov/common/archives/files/res_topics_ed_reform.pdf.
31. William S. Bush, *Who Gets a Childhood?: Race and Juvenile Justice in Twentieth Century Texas* (Athens, GA: The University of Georgia Press, 2010), 10.
32. Judith N. McArthur, "Woman's Christian Temperance Union," *Handbook of Texas Online* (June 2010), accessed March 22, 2016, http://www.tshaonline.org/handbook/online/articles/vaw01.
33. May Harper Baines, *A Story of Texas White Ribboners* (1935).
34. Judith N. McArthur, "Beauchamp, Jenny Bland," *Handbook of Texas Online* (March 2016), accessed March 22, 2016, http://www.tshaonline.org/handbook/online/articles/fbeaj.
35. McArthur,"Beauchamp, Jenny Bland."
36. Baines, *A Story of Texas White Ribboners*.
37. Bush, *Who Gets a Childhood?*
38. Bush, *Who Gets a Childhood?*
39. Bush, *Who Gets a Childhood?*
40. Bush, *Who Gets a Childhood?*
41. "State Training School," *Fort Worth Star-Telegram*, March 11, 1942.
42. Bush, *Who Get's a Childhood?*, 96.
43. William S. Bush, *Protecting Texas' Most Precious Resource: A History of Juvenile Justice Policy in Texas, Part 1* (Texas Criminal Justice Coalition, 2008).
44. Bush, *Who Gets a Childhood?*, 93.
45. Bush, *Protecting Texas' Most Precious Resource*, 35.
46. Bush, *Protecting Texas' Most Precious Resource*, 35.
47. Bush, *Who Gets a Childhood?*, 172.
48. Texas Sunset Advisory Commission, *Sunset Staff Review of The Texas Residential Construction Commission: Final Report* (July 2009), https://www.sunset.texas.gov/reviews-and-reports/agencies/texas-juvenile-probation-commission.
49. William Ecenbarger, *Kids for Cash: Two Judges, Thousands of Children, and a $2.6 Million Kickback Scheme* (New York: The New Press, 2012).
50. SB 653, "An act relating to abolishing the Texas Youth Commission and the Texas Juvenile Probation Commission and transferring the powers and duties of those agencies to the newly created Texas Juvenile Justice Department and to the functions of the independent ombudsman that serves the department," (2011), http://www.capitol.state.tx.us/tlodocs/82R/billtext/pdf/SB00653F.pdf.

Chapter 2

51. "Orphan Train Movement" (web page), Children's Aid New York, http://www.childrensaidsociety.org/about/history/orphan-trains.

52. "History and Timeline" (web page), Gladney Center for Adoption, http://adoptionsbygladney.com/about/our-heritage.

53. "History and Timeline," Gladney Center for Adoption.

54. Frank Burkett et al., *Beyond the Blue: The Lena Pope Home* (Lena Pope Home Inc., 2010).

55. "History" (web page), ACH Child and Family Services, https://achservices.org/about-ach/history/

56. Neilsen, *The Laws of Texas*, 13:137-140.

57. "Juvenile Court Bill: Open Session of Those Interested to be Held Friday," *Dallas Morning News*, December 10, 1906.

58. "Juvenile Court Bill: Judge Webb Congratulates Chief of Police Maddox," *Dallas Morning News*, April 7, 1907.

59. "Probation Boys Keep in Path: Report is Made to Secretary Travis of Juvenile Work," *Fort Worth Star-Telegram*, August 12, 1907.

60. P. Periwinkle, "Indorsement of Juvenile Courts," *Dallas Morning News*, February 24, 1908.

61. "Tarrant County Lowers Tax Levy: Travis to Stay in Fort Worth," *Dallas Morning News*, August 14, 1908.

62. "Terrell Praises Juvenile Court," *Fort Worth Star-Telegram*, July 18, 1908.

Chapter 3

63. "Father of Juvenile Courts Visits Texas: Dr. Orne Urges Industrial School for State," *Dallas Morning News*, March 25, 1909.

64. "Probation Boys Keep in Path," *Fort Worth Star-Telegram*, August 12, 1907.

65. P. Periwinkle, "Indorsement of Juvenile Courts."

66. "Armour Plan Approved: Officials of Packing House Assist Probation Officer in Solving Juvenile Court Problem," *Dallas Morning News*, September 21, 1907.

67. "EB Travis Going To Dallas: Fort Worth Man Will Take Charge of Juvenile Court Offenders There," *Dallas Morning News*, August 13, 1908.

68. "Tarrant County Lowers Tax Levy," *Dallas Morning News*, August 14, 1908.

69. "Women of Federation Name Juvenile Officer: William G. Leeman Begins Work among Boys of Dallas," *Dallas Morning News*, August 17, 1908.

70. "Tarrant Juvenile Court Abolished," *Dallas Morning News*, December 2, 1910.

71. Hans Peter Mareus Neilsen, *The Laws of Texas* (Austin, TX: Gammel Book Company, 1914), 16:226-227.

72. "900 Applications in for Job as County Probation Officer," *Fort Worth Star-Telegram*, May 25, 1913.

73. "Callaway Resigns as School Superintendent," *Fort Worth Star-Telegram*, July 1, 1913.

74. "Callaway Resigns," *Fort Worth Star-Telegram*.

75. "Callaway Resigns," *Fort Worth Star-Telegram*.

76. "Be a Companion to the Bad Boy: Callaway's Ideas of Reform," *Fort Worth Star-Telegram*, July 3, 1913.

77. "Be a Companion to the Bad Boy," *Fort Worth Star-Telegram*.

78. Neilsen, *The Laws of Texas*, 16:226-227.

79. "Be a Companion to the Bad Boy," *Fort Worth Star-Telegram*.

80. "Newsboys Leader Decries Taking Photographs 'Mugging,'" *Fort Worth Star-Telegram*, November 7, 1913; "'Williams Ignorant,' Callaway Retorts," *Fort Worth Star-Telegram*, November 9, 1913.

81. "UT Professor Cautions on Juvenile Work," *Fort Worth Star-Telegram*, November 14, 1913.

82. "Callaway Urges A Detention Home," *Fort Worth Star-Telegram*, August 3, 1913.

83. "Tarpley Named Probation Officer," *Dallas Morning News*, July 5, 1915.

84. "H. Tarpley to Lead Juveniles," *Dallas Morning News*, July 6, 1915, 4.

85. "H. Tarpley to Lead Juveniles," *Dallas Morning News*.

86. Tarrant County Juvenile Services, Juvenile Case Files, (1910-1923).

87. "Compulsory Attendance Officer Named in Fort Worth," *Dallas Morning News*, January 12, 1920.

88. "Roads Discussed by County Judges," *Dallas Morning News*, January 23, 1921.

89. "Hearing Held on Training School: Committee Questions Probation Officers and Former Inmates," *Dallas Morning News*, February 20, 1923.

90. "S.S. Ogilvie Chosen as County Probation Officer," *Dallas Morning News*, November 29, 1918.

91. "Verdict is Suicide in Ogilvie's Death," *Dallas Morning News*, November 2, 1932.

92. "Texas Probation Officers Perfect New Organization," *Dallas Morning News*, September 23, 1935.

93. "Pretty School Grounds Cut Child Delinquency, Tarrant Officials Learn," *Dallas Morning News*, July 23, 1935.

94. Martin Frey, "The Evolution of Juvenile Court Jurisdiction and Procedure in Texas," *Texas Tech Law Review* 1, (1970): 209, https://digitalcommons.law.utulsa.edu/cgi/viewcontent.cgi?referer=https://www.google.com/&httpsredir=1&article=1274&context=fac_pub.

95. Bush, *Who Gets a Childhood?*

96. "Rise in Delinquency," *Dallas Morning News*, March 27, 1943.

Chapter 4

97. "Tarrant Fills Probation Job," *Dallas Morning News*, December 7, 1946.

98. L. Ross Jr., in discussion with the author, April 24, 2011.

99. Ross, discussion.

100. Ross, discussion.

101. "Tarrant Fills Probation Job," *Dallas Morning News*.

102. Ross, discussion.

103. Ross, discussion.

104. Ross, discussion.

105. V. Herdman and J. Wood, in discussion with the author, April 14, 2011.

106. Ross, discussion.

107. Ross, discussion.

108. J. Wood, in discussion with the author, April 14, 2011.

109. C. Cockerell, in discussion with the author, May 4, 2011.

110. Wood, discussion.

111. Ross, discussion.

112. L. Willis, in discussion with the author, April 5, 2011.

113. "Parole Board Officer Blasts Commission," *Dallas Morning News*, June 13, 1977.

114. "County Juvenile Agency Wins National Award," *Dallas Morning News*, April 24, 1979.

115. E. Bark, "TV Film Crew Shoots the Works in Dallas," *Dallas Morning News*, February 3, 1981.

116. Willis, discussion.

117. P. Cromwell, *Probation Officer Training Manual* (Tarrant County Juvenile Services, 1977).

118. P. Cromwell, *Probation Officer Training Manual*.

119. P. Cromwell, *Probation Officer Training Manual*.

120. P. Gordon, "Cromwell Glad Name Is Cleared," *Dallas Morning News*, June 21, 1984.

121. Wood, discussion.

122. Wood, discussion.

123. Wood, discussion.

124. Wood, discussion.

125. Cockerell, discussion.

126. Cockerell, discussion.

127. Cockerell, discussion.

128. Cockerell, discussion.

129. Cockerell, discussion.

130. Cockerell, discussion.

131. Cockerell, discussion.

132. Youth Advocate Program (website), http://www.yapinc.org/WhoWeAre/OurHistory/tabid/488/Default.aspx.

133. Cockerell, discussion.

134. Cockerell, discussion.

135. Lena Pope Home (website), https://www.lenapope.org/lena-pope/about-us/our-history/.

136. Cockerell, discussion.

137. P. Thomas, in discussion with the author, May 6, 2012.

138. Thomas, discussion.

139. Thomas, discussion.

140. Betty Brink, "Thanks, But No Thanks: Turning Down Millions in State Money to Build Juvenile Boot Camps, Tarrant County Opted for a Different Approach—One That Works," *Dallas Observer*, September 27, 2001.

141. R. Mendel, "Less Hype, More Help: Reducing Juvenile Crime—What Works and What Doesn't?" American Youth Policy Forum, 2000.

142. Betty Brink, "Thanks, But No Thanks."

143. J. Wolfson and J. Hubner, "Unlocking the Future: Detention Reform in Juvenile Justice," Coalition for Juvenile Justice, 2003.

144. Wolfson and Hubner, "Unlocking the Future."

145. F. Hesselbein and M. Goldsmith, *The Leader of the Future 2: Visions, Strategies, and Practices for the New Era* (San Francisco: Jossey-Bass Publishing, 2006), 126.

146. Ronald Corbett, "Interviews with Two Leading Theorists of Leadership," *Corrections Management Quarterly* 3, no. 1 (1999).

147. "1 A MI Definition Principles & Approach V4 012911," https://www.umass.edu/studentlife/sites/default/files/documents/pdf/Motivational_Interviewing_Definition_Principles_Approach.pdf.

148. John Gordon, *Soup: A Recipe to Nourish Your Team and Culture* (Hoboken, NJ: John Wiley & Sons, 2010), 65.

149. B. Medlin, in discussion with the author, September 9, 2016.

Note: Paul Cromwell declined to be interviewed for this project.
Note: Randy Turner was interviewed for the project but declined publication.

Chapter 5

150. "Tarrant Juvenile Court Abolished," *Dallas Morning News*, December 2, 1910.

151. M. Frey, "The Evolution of Juvenile Court Jurisdiction and Procedure in Texas."

152. "B&PW Speaker at Fair Day Calls For 'Total Womanhood,'" *Dallas Morning News*, October 26, 1965.

153. E. Tyler (daughter of Scott Moore), in discussion with the author, April 5, 2011.

154. Tyler, discussion.

155. Tyler, discussion.

156. Tyler, discussion.

157. Tyler, discussion.

158. Tyler, discussion.

159. Cockerell, discussion.

160. Cockerell, discussion.

161.Boyd, in discussion with the author, July 9, 2012.

162."Gatesville Abuse and Committee: Midnight Raiders," *Fort Worth Star-Telegram*, January 6, 1969.

163. S. Fuller, in discussion with the author, April 28, 2011.

164. Boyd, discussion.

165. Boyd, discussion.

166. "Judge Sends Fewer Youths to Gatesville State School," *Dallas Morning News*, September 19, 1969.

167. "Judge Sends Fewer Youths," *Dallas Morning News*.

168. Boyd, discussion.

169. Boyd, discussion.

170. Boyd, discussion.

171. Boyd, discussion.

172. Boyd, discussion.

173. Boyd, discussion.

174. Boyd, discussion.

175. Boyd, discussion.

176. Boyd, discussion.

177. Boyd, discussion.

178. Boyd, discussion.

179. Boyd, discussion.

180. Boyd, discussion.

181. Boyd, discussion.

182. Boyd, discussion.
183. Boyd, discussion.
184. Boyd, discussion.
185. Boyd, discussion.
186. Boyd, discussion.
187. Boyd, discussion.
188. Boyd, discussion.
189. Boyd, discussion.
190. Boyd, discussion.
191. Boyd, discussion.
192. Boyd, discussion.
193. Boyd, discussion.
194. Boyd, discussion.
195. Boyd, discussion.
196. Boyd, discussion.
197. E. Smith, in discussion with the author, May 27, 2011.
198. Smith, discussion.
199. Smith, discussion.
200. Smith, discussion.
201. Smith, discussion.
202. Smith, discussion.
203. K. Brown, in discussion with the author, July 6, 2011.
204. Brown, discussion.
205. J. Teel, in discussion with the author, September 7, 2016.

Note: Ernie Bates did not respond to requests to be interviewed for this project.

Chapter 6
206. Bob Dawson, oral history interview by P. Hazel, the University of Texas Law School Foundation.
207. Shaw and Penn, "Texas State Supplement to Chapter 5 of Cox, S.M. et al."
208. T. Goodman, in discussion with the author, May 25, 2011.
209. Goodman, discussion.
210. Goodman, discussion.
211. Goodman, discussion.
212. Goodman, discussion.
213. Goodman, discussion.
214. University of Texas at Austin School of Law (website), "In Memoriam Professor Robert O. Dawson (1939- 2005)," https://news.utexas.edu/2005/02/28/law-professor-robert-o-dawson-dies-at-age-65/.
215. UT Austin School of Law, "In memoriam Professor Robert O. Dawson."
216. UT Austin School of Law, "In memoriam Professor Robert O. Dawson."
217. Dawson, interview.
218. Dawson, interview.
219. R. Shaw, in discussion with the author, June 17, 2011.
220. Shaw, discussion.
221. Shaw, discussion.

222. Shaw, discussion.
223. Shaw, discussion.
224. Shaw, discussion.

Chapter 7
225. Boyd, discussion.
226. Cockerell, discussion.
227. Goodman, discussion.
228. Cockerell, discussion.
229. Austin L. Porterfield, *Youth in Trouble: Studies in Delinquency and Despair* (Fort Worth, TX: Leo Potishman Foundation, 1946).
230. Austin L. Porterfield, "The Complainant in Juvenile Court," *Sociology and Social Research* 28, no. 3 (January 1944): 180-81.
231. Henry Adams, *The Education of Henry Adams: An Autobiography* (Boston: The Riverside Press, 1907).

Chapter 8
232. A. Porterfield and L. Potishman, "Detention Center Editorial Opinions," *Fort Worth Star-Telegram*, May 19, 1947.
233. R. Miller, "County's Juvenile Setup Commended," *Dallas Morning News*, January 19, 1955.
234. "Detention Center Urged for Fort Worth," *Dallas Morning News*, November 16, 1967; "Tarrant Group to Visit Detention Areas," *Dallas Morning News*, March 16, 1968; "Judge Hits County on Juvenile Center," *Dallas Morning News*, November 22, 1969.
235. "Detention Home Urged for Tarrant Juveniles" *Dallas Morning News*, December 4, 1966.
236. Paul F. Cromwell and J. M. Townley, "Tarrant County Youth Center: Innovations in Program and Funding," *Juvenile and Family Court Journal* 32, no. 1 (February 1981): 51–57.
237. Paul F. Cromwell and J. M. Townley, "Tarrant County Youth Center," 51-57.
238. C. Freund, "U.S. Team Urges 'New Look' In Child Care, Raps Officials," *Dallas Morning News*, May 13, 1967.
239. C. Freund, "'New Look' in Child Care."
240. "Vote Sought On Building Youth Home," *Dallas Morning News*, May 14, 1967.
241. "Body Found by Jailers," *Dallas Morning News*, January 2, 1968; "Boy's Death Spurs Drive for Center," *Dallas Morning News*, January 27, 1968.
242. "Tarrant Agrees On Center Site," *Dallas Morning News*, March 22, 1968.
243. "Tarrant Picks Juvenile Center Site," *Dallas Morning News*, May 11, 1968.
244. Texas State Historical Association, "The County Poor Farm System in Texas," *The Southwestern Historical Quarterly* 93 (July 1989), http://texashistory.unt.edu/ark:/67531/metapth101213/
245. Constitution of the State of Texas, Article XII, Section 26. Adopted by the Constitutional Convention convened under the reconstruction acts of Congress passed March 2, 1867, and the acts supplementary thereto: to be submitted for ratification or rejection at an election to take place on the first Monday of July, 1869. Austin, Texas; printed at the Daily Republican Office. 1869. Winkler-Friend 2121.

246. Texas State Historical Association, "The County Poor Farm System in Texas."

247. Texas State Historical Association, "The County Poor Farm System in Texas."

248. Texas State Historical Association, "The County Poor Farm System in Texas."

249. "New Site Selected for Detention Center," *Dallas Morning News*, December 9, 1969.

250. Arlington Turnpike document or article

251. "Tarrant Juvenile Center: Woodworking Shop, Beauty Center Planned," *Dallas Morning News*, May 13, 1968.

252. Interview with a member of the Dirty Seven, 2013.

253. C. Freund, "Funds Spent Without Contract: Lack of Responsibility, Sloppy Bookkeeping Cited," *Dallas Morning News*, March 22, 1980.

254. C. Freund, "Funds Spent Without Contract."

255. B. West, in discussion with the author, June 16, 2011.

256. Interview with S. Williams, June 23, 2011; Tarrant County contract with Baker Funeral Home (March 2, 1949); Claim of Baker Funeral Home for rent on office space for asst. probation (negro) officer.

257. R. Woodert, in discussion with the author, December 2, 2012.

258. A. Briones, in discussion with the author, May 10, 2012

Chapter 9

259. Julian Mack, "The Juvenile Court," *Harvard Law Review* 23, no. 2 (December 1909): 120.

260. M. Moncrief, in discussion with the author, June 9, 2001.

Chapter 10 - Conclusion

261. The Associated Press, "As New York Prepares to Close More Youth Detention Facilities, Violence in Them Rises," The *Post Standard* (June 2011), http://www.syracuse.com/news/index.ssf/2011/06/as_new_york_prepares_to_close.html.

262. G. Carrion, in discussion with the author, June 30, 2011.

263. The Associated Press, "As New York Prepares to Close More Youth Detention Facilities."

264. Jim Collins, *Good to Great: Why Some Companies Make the Leap . . . and Others Don't* (New York; Harper Collins Publishing, 2011).

265. Nell Burnstein, *Burning Down the House: The End of Juvenile Prison* (New York: The New Press, 2014), 274.

Index

Photo by Casa Davila Photography

About the Author

Greg Sumpter has been pursuing the dream of justice for young people for over a quarter century and has served as a juvenile justice professional for twenty-three years. He began his juvenile justice career in rural Arkansas, served for twenty-two years in juvenile justice in Tarrant County, in the fifteenth largest city in the US, and has recently accepted a position as the assistant director for Grayson County Juvenile Services. Sumpter is a member of MINT (Motivational Interviewing Network of Trainers) and currently serves on the Professional Development Committee. A Trust Based Relational Intervion (TBRI) practioner, he has previously served as chair and vice chair of the Texas Motivational Interviewing Cooperative (TMIC) and was a cofounder of the Motivational Interviewing Training Academy (MITA). Sumpter completed a master's program with a management focus and is a PhD candidate in leadership studies. He lives in Denton, Texas, and is the father of two high school boys.

CPSIA information can be obtained
at www.ICGtesting.com
Printed in the USA
BVHW080813060219
539571BV00003B/69/P